The Clever Student:
A Guide to Getting the Most from Your Professors

Anita E. Kelly, PhD
Professor of Psychology, University of Notre Dame

Corby Publications
Notre Dame, Indiana

The Clever Student:
A Guide to Getting the Most from Your Professors
Copyright © 2010 Anita E. Kelly, PhD

10 9 8 7 6 5 4 3 2 1

ISBN 978-0-9819605-8-6

Manufactured in the United States of America

Published by Corby Books
A Division of Corby Publishing
P.O. Box 93
Notre Dame, Indiana 46556
(574) 784-3482
www.corbypublishing.com

Table of Contents

Introduction
Your Social Intelligence Can Boost Your Grades vii
Chapter 1
Assess Yourself – Are You Socially Intelligent in the
Classroom? 1
Chapter 2
How Your Professors Think 17
Chapter 3
Showing Your Professors "I'm Here to Learn!" 27
Chapter 4
Handling Excuses for Missed Classes or Exams 33
Chapter 5
Your First-Rate Class Participation 41
Chapter 6
Writing a Great Paper *for that Professor* 49
Chapter 7
Differences between Small Colleges versus
Universities. 61
Chapter 8
Handling Conflicts over Your Grades 67
Chapter 9
Eleven Things to Avoid 79
Chapter 10
What to Do If You Are Accused of Cheating 87
Chapter 11
Overcoming Depression. 95
Chapter 12
Getting Your Professors to Write You Amazing Letters
of Recommendation. 103
Chapter 13
Your Future Is So Bright. .121
References 125

This book is dedicated to Pascal Lavallée,
my Clever husband.

INTRODUCTION
Your Social Intelligence Can Boost Your Grades

It's 20 minutes into the spring final exam. Two graduate students stroll into my classroom, plunk into their seats, drop their backpacks, and pull out their pens. Their classmates, who have been dutifully scribbling out answers the whole time, look up with the same expression of puzzlement as must be on my own face. One of the late comers casually explains that their breakfast ran over. That event kicked off what turned out to be six years of struggling in graduate school for both those students.

What went wrong for them? You might say that it was their lateness and that they were destined for failure because they lacked the punctuality necessary to succeed. You might say that it was their lack of motivation – obviously anyone who shows up that late for a final exam must not be too excited about his or her studies. Or you might say that they lacked the conscientiousness necessary for the rigors of graduate school.

But I don't think any one of those things was what really hurt them. What really hurt them was a lack of practical intelligence that was needed to handle their professors effectively. Research has shown that students' practical ability in graduate school can predict their professors' ratings of their competence far better than their GRE scores.[1] This practical ability includes accurately reading the expectations of professors and flexibly responding to those expectations. An example of such flexibility is knowing that sometimes it is much better to spin the truth rather than to tell the complete, honest truth.[2] Practically intelligent people recognize this point and don't hurt others, including their professors, with completely honest and inappropriate excuses. These two students didn't seem to realize that acting so casual about being late for a final was far worse than being late itself.

Here's another example that demonstrates this point before I go into why I am writing this book. Once, an undergraduate showed up at my office the day after my midterm exam and said she had missed the test because she had gotten herself very sick by drinking too much the night before the test. She went into detail about how she had been vomiting exactly when the other students were taking the test.

Now you are probably thinking that this student was very sweet in telling me the whole truth. And to some extent, I agree with you. However, she could have simply told me that she had been throwing up during the test and shown me a medical excuse from the infirmary. Then I could have just given her the test with no questions asked. But those extra details about her drinking put me in the tough spot of trying to do what would be most fair to the rest of the class who hadn't gotten drunk the night before the test and had taken it on time. The details made me consider not giving her a make-up test, whereas I could have instantly agreed that any student who was throwing up deserved a make-up test.

In contrast to the actions of this student, practically intelligent students put themselves in the shoes of their professors. They realize that professors want to be consistent – and thus fair – with their students. We professors want to avoid making exceptions for students who bend the rules that we have laid out for them in the syllabus. (In case you're wondering, I did give her the exam after she produced a medical excuse from the infirmary.)

So why am I writing this book? It's because I want to help you get great grades and letters of recommendation *and* get along seamlessly with your professors. You and/or your parents are spending ridiculous amounts of money on your college education (by the way, your professors see very little of that money). Naturally, I want you to get the most value, both emotionally and academically, out of your college experience. I often have been dumbfounded by how students who are so academically intelligent and so well-prepared for their college studies can be so – er – clueless about what to say to their professors. For instance, the majority of students don't seem to realize that they can get their professors to dislike them instantly by simply raising their hand in class and innocently asking, "Do we really have to study all this material on X for the test?" Another common innocent slip is calling your female professors "Mrs. X" instead of "Dr. X" or "Professor X", when almost every single one of us has earned a PhD. We likely wouldn't be "Mrs." anyhow because we probably kept our pre-married names. (I ask my students to call me Anita but recommend that you call your professors "Dr. X", unless they ask you to use some other title.)

Perhaps even more surprising is that some students will actually get up from even the front row during a lecture and march out of the room to take a phone call or go to the bathroom. One senior colleague recently told me that he was so stunned and distracted when a female student left his lecture that he started stammering over his lecture material. He seethingly told me that she "was incredibly disrespectful." Was she disrespectful?

The Clever Student

I don't think so. What is happening in college campuses across the U.S. is that students are coming to see themselves as consumers, as opposed to pupils, of their college courses. They see their professors as providing a service for which they or their parents have paid in full. That student who walked out of the lecture probably had no idea how enraging her behavior was. She simply made a decision not to use all the services from the professor that were bought and paid for! How do I know that she was thinking this? It's because I have asked my current students why they walk out on lectures, and they've told me that it's because they are the consumers and have a right to leave. The problem is not merely that students today hold this belief. The problem is also that their professors do not share this belief. Professors across the country still see themselves as being the rulers of the classroom and see their students as having the privilege of learning from them. If students enrage their professors, they put themselves at risk for poorer grades. And grades are just as important, if not more important, to students today than they were in the past.

Students who act like consumers instead of pupils are probably particularly bothersome to more senior professors who are used to getting respect. However, just because your professors drive brown 2002 Honda Accords or used silver Toyota Camrys and wear rubber-soled shoes under pants that are too short doesn't mean that you can check your socially appropriate behaviors at the classroom door. That is, not if you want great grades and letters of recommendation.

But here's the deal. Research has demonstrated that people can learn to be more practically and socially intelligent.[3] By reading this book, you can learn how to apply this intelligence to getting the best out of your professors in such a way that will make both them and you feel good. More important, your boost in these non-academic kinds of intelligence will make them more likely to give you good grades and write you very strong letters of recommendation that are essential for your job or graduate-school placement.

In case you are thinking that this guide sounds a bit manipulative, let me be clear about something. We professors, consciously or unconsciously, want our students to manage us well. You're right – this is a strange thing for a professor to say. It's strange because in academia, in contrast to the corporate world, everybody is supposed to be genuine and honest. No matter what field they are in, professors see themselves as pursuing the truth in their research. This pursuit spills over to the classroom where students are supposed to be genuine, engaged, and critical.

But these are just ideals. Professors are humans first, and humans have certain norms for interacting that require cooperation. Professors might say they want defiant or irreverent students, yet they really want students to follow their critical agenda. The clever, successful students cooperate by being critical of course material, as opposed to being critical of the professor and his or her teaching skills.

I admit, however, that we professors can be very confusing about our critical agenda in the classroom. For instance, at a recent cocktail party on campus, a colleague in the humanities told me that he wants the students in his seminars "to do precisely the opposite" of what he tells them to do. I responded to his confusing statement by saying, "But you want them to criticize the course material, which at a meta-level, is precisely what you *want* them to do." He thought for a second, and then agreed by saying, "That meta-level is a bit of a sticky wicket, isn't it?" By the way, *meta* means above.

This example illustrates how important it is to understand what your professors really mean at a higher level when they say that they want you to disagree with them. No professor, in truth, wants a student to do the opposite of his or her wishes. That notion doesn't even make sense. But virtually all professors want the students in their seminars to be critical of the course material. If you understand how professors think and follow the norms for interacting with them flexibly and seamlessly, your professors will be pulling for you to do well. This means, for example, that if you are in between two grades at the end of the semester, your professor might just give you that little shove to the higher grade.

Perhaps you are wondering why a psychology professor at Notre Dame and former psychotherapist would write such a book. The reason is that I understand and feel for students who don't know some of the social norms for relating to their professors. After all, where would you get this knowledge? College life and expectations are so different from the rules in high school, particularly if your high school is one where some or most of the students do not continue on to college or if you went to high school overseas. My own experience was one of culture shock attending Northwestern University, having come from a middle-class public high school in upstate New York. I both smile and cringe when I look back on those days when I would wear my purple Northwestern varsity sweats to class as if to say to my professors, "I am an athlete! I don't belong to this class of fine academically-oriented students." It wasn't until much later that I discovered the research which demonstrates that professors often have a negative bias against college athletes.[4] If I knew then what I know now, I would have kept those sweats out of sight (except for cold practices, of course)!

Another question you might have is, "Why should you bother listening to me?" Well, for one thing, I have been studying and teaching college courses on personality and impression management for 18 years. Another is that I have ended up in service roles here on Notre Dame's campus that have put me in a good position to see the (often innocent) mistakes college students make that get them on the wrong side of their professors' good graces. For example, I have served and am serving as Chair of our Institutional Review Board (which makes judgments about the ethics of research projects), as Co-Chair of our college's Honesty Committee, and as the Sexual Harassment Ombudsperson. All of these service roles have taught me fascinating things about what college students today expect and believe about their campus life that can get them into trouble. In addition, last year I served as a Teaching Fellow at Notre Dame and gave workshops on teaching to my fellow professors and graduate-student instructors. I learned a great deal about what they find difficult about teaching and what they do to try to reach students in the classroom.

In this book, I start out by providing assessments of how socially intelligent in the classroom you are relative to other college students. Your scores represent merely a starting point of your social intelligence to give you a sense of how much work you will need to put into this process of honing your skill in interacting with your professors (Chapter 1).

Then, in Chapter 2, I offer insights on how your professors think and what motivates them to be college professors. Their motivations vary depending on whether they are oriented toward teaching or research. You probably have spent little or no time thinking about how your professors think. After all, you have your friends, your diet, your finances, your parents, and your lack of time to exercise and study to worry about. But isn't a huge part of the reason why you're in college that you're trying to land a great job or place in graduate, medical, or law school? You need really strong letters of recommendations and very solid grades to do it. This chapter is devoted to getting inside the heads of your professors so that you can maximize both.

In Chapter 3, I offer suggestions for how you can convey to your professors that you are there to learn (as opposed to there solely as a means to an end). After all, nothing fires up a teacher more than feeling that we are sharing our passion for knowledge with our students.

In Chapter 4, I offer specific pointers for how to handle excuses for missed classes or exams. Chapters 5 and 6 address how to excel at class participation, even if you are shy, and how to write first-rate papers for each particular professor. Chapter 7 addresses differences between small colleges and universities, and between undergraduate and graduate school. Chapter 8 answers the tricky question, how do I handle conflicts over my grades with my professors? Chapter 9 lays out eleven common things that students do to shoot themselves in the foot and that are important to avoid doing in college.

Chapter 10 addresses something you might not think is important now, but can be devastating if it happens to you: what to do if you are accused of cheating. Often stu-

Introduction

dents take their professor's accusation to their college's honesty committee, only to discover that their penalty ends up much worse after the committee hears the case. Chapter 11 deals with what to do if you become depressed during a given semester. Your college has resources that can help get over depression much more quickly than if you do nothing to treat it.

Finally, the book concludes with Chapters 12 and 13 addressing your excellent future prospects and how to get your professors to write you amazing letters of recommendation to send you down your bright path. You can be that Clever Student, who is very socially and practically intelligent, that all your professors talk about and appreciate!

You'll notice as you read the chapters that I share a good deal about my personal reactions to students and their behaviors in the classroom. I share these with you because I have lived this role of professor and believe that your professors often will have reactions that are similar to mine. So, if you can really get inside my head, then this might help you get inside the heads of your own professors.

My stance in writing this book is to be like an informed coach and a cheerleader in helping you use your social intelligence to succeed in college. As you read, please post your reactions and comments on my blog at TheCleverStudent.com. I would love to hear from you!

Assess Yourself
Are You Socially Intelligent in the Classroom?

Chapter 1

You have no-doubt heard the terms practical intelligence and social intelligence. Practical intelligence is a broad term that refers to our ability to adapt to, shape, and select everyday environments.[5] Social intelligence is more specific in that it refers to our ability to interact with and manage people effectively and adapt to various situations involving them. These concepts contrast with academic intelligence, which is largely associated with the extensiveness of our vocabulary and how we score on standardized tests like the SAT.

What's interesting is that even though colleges emphasize SAT scores in admissions decisions, Professor Robert Sternberg, the leading expert on practical intelligence, says that practical intelligence is even more crucial to real-world success than is academic intelligence. An example comes from a study conducted during the 1980s on a group of men who were experts at laying correct odds on race horses and picking the winners. These 30 men would be considered geniuses for all practical purposes because they could gather the relevant information and make extremely complex computations involving as many as seven variables on the spot to correctly calculate the anticipated speed of the horses. Yet when researchers measured their academic intelligence with an IQ test, the men were simply average, scoring right around 100.[6]

Another important discovery that Professor Sternberg and other researchers have made is that practical and social intelligence are only very modestly positively related to academic intelligence. The relationship between social intelligence and academic intelligence is so small that if we were to measure a group of individuals' IQ scores, these scores would account for only about 9% of the variation in the individuals' social intelligence. This fact probably fits your observation that professionals like lawyers and doctors can sometimes be super-smart academically but yet socially inept. In fact, research has shown that although scores on the MCAT (i.e., the standardized test used for medical school admission) are a good predictor of academic performance in medical school, they do not predict the essential clinical performance of medical students.[7]

Moreover, many studies have shown that a student's practical and social intelligence can predict both the grades that students earn and how teachers rate them.[3,5] This is good news for you since you are reading this book, and research has shown that these kinds of non-academic intelligence can be learned and are improved through education.[3]

So let's get into the specifics of how socially intelligent in the classroom you are right now. Keep in mind that practical intelligence and social intelligence are basically the same thing in the classroom because other students and professors are involved in every situation. Professor Sternberg claims that practical intelligence must be assessed in a specific context because people can be very practically and socially intelligent in one context, such as in the military, but not so intelligent in another, such as in a playground full of young children.[5]

When researchers asked people to list features that made up their own personal concept of social intelligence, the participants listed the following as most essential:[8]

(a) Has extensive knowledge of rules and norms in human relations.
(b) Is good at dealing with people.
(c) Understands and is good at taking the perspective of other people.
(d) Adapts well in social situations. Is open to new experiences, ideas, and values.
(e) Is warm and caring.

It would be difficult to imagine that an academic intelligence test like the SAT could measure anything like the features on this list. Thus, I had to develop a test of social intelligence in the classroom. I did it by using this list of features that everyday people associate with social intelligence. I then created social intelligence questions to capture these features and gave these questions to samples of Notre Dame undergraduates. For the test you will take next, the more advanced students (i.e., those in a senior psychology seminar versus those in a general undergraduate psychology course) got significantly higher scores. When you are done taking the test, you will be able to see how your scores compare with those of samples of Notre Dame undergraduates.

The Clever Student

Keep in mind that this test is very challenging and that your scores represent only a starting point. My goal is for you to be able to score 100% after you are done reading this book. The reason it is so important for you to score well is that the better you can understand your college environment and your professors' point of view, the better you will be able to adapt and succeed in college. If you can figure out what your professor wants and expects *without having to ask*, this is even better than having to ask. I know you think that asking questions makes you look earnest and hardworking. But in actuality, you run the risk of looking unintelligent or even annoying your usually-overworked professor by asking questions that are completely obvious. For example, if a professor says that his office hours are only in the mornings, don't ask if you can see him in the late afternoon.

So give yourself 15 uninterrupted minutes to take the following test. You'll notice that there are lots of questions on understanding your professors' rank and position in your college. The reason knowledge about their status is critical to your success is that if you can discern which of your professors have tenure, and thus job security and higher status, you can understand which ones will have more time for you and which ones will write you letters of recommendation that carry the most weight (they are usually not the same people).

Assess Yourself

Test of Social Intelligence in the College Classroom

Choose the best answer. Regarding the questions about your personality, please answer the questions honestly and consider your behavior in the classroom context.

1. What is a key difference between the doctoral degrees of the PhD and MD?
   a. A PhD candidate must produce a thesis or dissertation of his or her own original academic research to graduate.
   b. An MD candidate must produce a thesis or dissertation of his or her own original academic research to graduate.
   c. The MD is the highest degree that can be earned.
   d. Earning a PhD always requires earning a master's degree first.

2. How much training does a professor typically get on how to teach?
   a. None.
   b. A one-semester graduate course on teaching.
   c. At least one year of graduate coursework on teaching.
   d. Four years of supervision and graduate coursework on teaching.

3. A typical syllabus is most like which of the following?
   a. A general flexible outline of what the students can expect in the course.
   b. A contract with details about course objectives and firm due dates for exams or papers.

    c. A description of the professor's background and qualifications.

    d. A history of how the course was developed and what the course objectives are.

4. Your favorite professor invites you and 3 other undergraduate students over for dinner. You go and have a wonderful time. Which of the following is the most appropriate thing to do afterward?

    a. Repay the favor by making the professor dinner at your house.

    b. Buy a generous gift and give it to the professor.

    c. Send the professor a thank you card.

    d. Do nothing in particular.

5. What is the difference between a college and a university?

    a. Colleges are less prestigious than universities.

    b. Universities cost more than colleges.

    c. Universities tend to be public; colleges tend to be private.

    d. Universities necessarily have graduate programs, whereas colleges may or may not have them.

6. Order the following in terms of lowest to highest rank:

    a. Assistant professor, associate professor, professor, endowed professor.

    b. Associate professor, assistant professor, professor, endowed professor.

    c. Endowed professor, associate professor, assistant professor, professor.

    d. Assistant professor, associate professor, professor, endowed professor.

7. **What of the following ranks does not have tenure?**
   a. Associate professor.
   b. Assistant professor.
   c. Professor.
   d. Endowed professor.

8. **Tenure for a professor is most like which of the following?**
   a. 10 years of service.
   b. Job security.
   c. Job prestige.
   d. Salary bonus.

9. **How long does it typically take for a professor to earn tenure?**
   a. 1 year
   b. 3 years
   c. 6 years.
   d. 10 years.

10. **What percentage of professors in the humanities and sciences have a PhD?**
   a. Approximately 100 percent
   b. Approximately 75 percent
   c. Approximately 50 percent
   d. Approximately 20 percent

11. **You are in a seminar of 17 students. You need to go to the bathroom. What is the most appropriate course of action?**
   a. You get up and leave to use the bathroom and then come back.

b. You get up and leave to use the bathroom but don't come back.
c. You raise your hand and ask permission to go.
d. You wait for the end of the class period to go.

12. What is the difference between a seminar and a course?
   a. Courses place more emphasis on student participation during class time.
   b. Seminars are easier to get good grades in.
   c. Seminars are usually offered only for a few weeks, whereas courses are usually a whole semester long.
   d. Seminars are more discussion based.

13. The professor for your philosophy seminar says that he will evaluate your in-class performance by how good your critical comments are. This means that you should be
   a. critical of both the professor's teaching style and the assigned readings during class because professors love students who aren't afraid to criticize them.
   b. critical of the assigned readings but not the professor's teaching style during class.
   c. cooperative and avoid criticizing either the readings or the professor both during class and in your papers.
   d. mostly silent during class and save your criticisms for your papers.

14. The average salary for a full-time U.S. college professor (who has had 9 years of college at the graduate and undergraduate levels) is around
   a. $52,000
   b. $62,000

c. $75,000

d. $95,000

15. Which of the following best characterizes your personality in class?

a. Friendly and warm.

b. Stand-offish and cold.

c. Neutral. Not particularly warm or cold when compared with other students.

d. Confident and ready to complain when necessary.

16. How far in advance of when your letter of recommendation is due should you ask your professor to write you one?

a. 1 week

b. 2 weeks

c. 4 weeks

d. 2 months

17. Imagine that your favorite professor Dr. Alex Jones, who all the students agree teaches extremely well, does not get tenure. What is the best explanation for that?

a. He did not publish enough.

b. He did not get along well with other faculty.

c. The university ran out of funds to support him.

d. He was too familiar with students and was seen as a sexual harassment threat.

18. What does a typical professor at a major university do in the summer?

a. Write grant proposals or scientific articles and books.

b. Prepare for the fall semester's teaching.

c. Teach courses for summer school.
d. They have the summer off.

19. How is a typical professor's time divided at a large university?
a. 50-60% teaching, 30-40% research, and 10-20% service.
b. 50-60% research, 30-40% teaching, and 10-20% service.
c. 50-60% service 30-40% teaching, and 10-20% research.
d. 50-60% research, 30-40% service, and 10-20% teaching.

20. Your professor tells you that your mid-term paper is to be 8 pages. This means that
a. It should be exactly 8 pages.
b. It should be at least 8 pages, but longer is even better.
c. It can be 7 and a half pages, as long as the paper ends on page 8.
d. A or B is right, depending on the professor.

21. Your professor tells the seminar at the beginning of the semester that class participation based on discussion of the readings is worth a third of the grade. This typically means that
a. Simply talking about the topic as much or more than other students will earn you an A for participation.
b. You can show up for every class period on time and not say anything and expect at least a B for participation.
c. You need to make insightful comments tied to the readings on a fairly regular basis to get an A.
d. You can show up for most of the classes and not say anything and expect at least a B for participation.

22. Imagine that you are finishing your first year of graduate school. Your academic advisor tells you that your grades don't matter and to focus on your research. Which of the following are you most likely to do?

  a. Focus on your research and do the minimum to pass your courses with a B.
  b. Do your best to get As in all your classes.
  c. Focus exclusively on your research and allow yourself to fail some of your classes.
  d. Ask other professors for their advice, in case your own professor is out of line with the norms in your department.

23. Which of the following best characterizes you?

  a. You are a procrastinator and don't finish projects on time.
  b. You finish projects, but barely on time.
  c. You start lots of projects, but don't finish many of them.
  d. You finish projects on time.
  e. You finish projects ahead of schedule.

24. Your professor tells you that you need to be critical of the course material in your paper. Your reaction is typically most like which of the following? (Be honest!)

  a. You summarize the material only because you have no idea how to be critical.
  b. You come up with ideas you think your professor will agree with.
  c. You come up with original criticisms of the course material.

    d. You ask a smart friend in the class what she thinks and try to recapture what she says in your paper.

25. Your professor tells you that in-class participation is worth a third of your grade. Your reaction is likely to be which of the following?
    a. Positive. You are so extraverted, you can talk your way to an A without doing the reading.
    b. Negative. You find it hard to say anything in class.
    c. Positive. You love to read and insights come easily to you. You are willing and able to share.
    d. Positive. You don't want to spend that much time writing really great papers, and your class participation grade can help offset any poor paper grades.

26. While sitting in a large lecture hall when your professor is lecturing you usually do which of the following?
    a. Day dream. You can always get the notes from somebody else later.
    b. Nod and act interested while diligently taking notes.
    c. Diligently take notes but make no special effort to look interested.
    d. Look bored and occasionally check the clock while taking notes.

27. A particular professor rubs you the wrong way. He seems arrogant and condescending. You respond by
    a. showing him up during class time by pointing out mistakes in his lectures.
    b. acting polite and respectful despite your disdain.
    c. skipping class and showing up late more than usual.

d. reporting him to his department chairperson during the semester.

e. looking bored and refusing to answer questions during class time.

28. A discussion of SAT scores comes up during a seminar on personality and intelligence testing. Your recommendation for a fellow male student who didn't score well on the SAT is to

a. admit his poor test score to the class. Professors will appreciate such honesty and see it as a sign of maturity.

b. avoid mentioning his poor test score. Professors can be judgmental about poor scores.

c. admit or not admit his scores because it doesn't matter either way. Nobody places much value on those tests anyhow.

d. talk about how badly a friend of yours did on the test.

29. Your professor asks you to call her by her first name. You respond by

a. continuing to use the title Dr or Professor before her last name out of respect.

b. not using any name because it makes you uncomfortable to use her first name.

c. continuing to call her Mrs. before her last name out of respect.

d. calling her by her first name.

30. For large lecture courses you

a. always show up early

b. always show up right on time.

    c. usually show up on time, but are late once in a while.

    d. show up late on a regular basis.

31. For large lecture courses you
    a. always sit in the front row
    b. always sit in the back.
    c. always sit in the middle.
    d. sit anywhere you can get a seat.

32. Imagine your girlfriend or boyfriend breaks up with you right before a huge exam and you are totally distracted by this. What should you do?
    a. Call and email the professor immediately and tell her that you are too distracted to concentrate on the exam because of the breakup and ask for a make-up test.
    b. Take the test and hope to do your best anyhow. If you can't concentrate, then after the test ask the professor for a make-up exam.
    c. Skip the test. Call and email the professor the next day to tell her what happened and ask for a make-up exam.
    d. Skip the test. Have your parents call the professor the next day to tell her what happened and ask for a make-up exam.

33. Compliments about how great a professor teaches are likely to have what impact on your professor?
    a. The professor will see you as a brown noser.
    b. The professor will like you more.
    c. The professor will see you as less intelligent than a more critical student.

    d. The professor will not care one way or another about
      your compliments.

ANSWERS TO THE 33 QUESTIONS:

1.a. 2.a. 3.b. 4.c. 5.d. 6.a 7.b. 8.b. 9.c. 10.a. 11.d. 12.d.
13.b 14.a. 15.a. 16.c. 17.a 18.a. 19.b. 20.d. 21.c. 22.a. 23.e. 24.c.
25.c. 26.b. 27.b. 28.b. 29.d. 30.a. 31.a. 32.a. 33.b.

Look at these answers and see how many you got
right. The Notre Dame undergraduates I tested who were
mostly sophomores and juniors got 17 out of the 33 right,
with two-thirds of the group falling between a score of 14
and 21. If you fell in this range then you are right on par
with students at a premier institution. If you found yourself getting fewer than 14 right, don't worry because by the
time you read all the chapters you will be acing this test!
Note that a sample of seniors in a psychology seminar got
an average of a whopping 21 correct. This finding that the
seniors did better than the broader group of undergraduates is consistent with previous research that, as mentioned
earlier, has shown that social intelligence can be increased
through education.[3] The next chapter gives insights on how
your professors think, and thus addresses all those questions about how to behave in their classrooms.

How Your Professors Think

Chapter 2

"This is silly."

These were the words my professor had scribbled in red in the margin next to an argument for C+ paper that I wrote for an undergraduate law course. Okay, so I had written the paper in one night and had run out of time to go to the law library downtown to do my research for it. But did I really deserve the words *this is silly*?

Just last year, I heard a young professor tell a group of graduate students that what they had been presenting all semester "was just fluff" as he made an airy gesture with both hands. The students look crushed, but none of the others professors or students said anything because we were all so dumbfounded.

Why do professors say such seemingly cruel things to their students? Don't we realize how much power we have to hurt with our words?

WE ARE NOT TEACHERS BY TRAINING

I believe that there are two main, inter-related reasons why professors can seem so heartless and critical at times.

The first reason is that most of us have had absolutely no training on how to teach. No one has ever taught us that berating or belittling students is completely off limits. You may think that college professors are "teachers", but actually, teaching is only a fraction of what we do.

The second reason is that what we are taught to do is research. As part of our research training, we are taught to seek truths and meaning, and to think critically. Critical thinking is prized, and then we find ourselves wanting our students to learn to think critically too. Unfortunately, what ends up happening is that professors often confuse trying to teach critical thinking with being critical. For many professors, if they are not critical of their students, they are falling short of some preeminent standard.

I'm fairly certain that what motivated the young professor who told the students that their work was "fluff" was that he was trying to push them to achieving higher standards with their research. To him, not confronting the students would be tantamount to maintaining a low status quo.

As you're reading this, you are probably thinking about some wonderfully supportive professors you've had who would never say such critical things. In fact, I had such a professor at Northwestern. He taught me my very favorite course that influenced me to have a career in psychology. He was passionate about the course material, dynamic as a lecturer, careful about grading, and spent lots of time with the students in his class. Imagine how stunned I was to learn during my senior year that the best professor I had ever had was leaving Northwestern because he was denied tenure. What?! I was totally confused. He sadly explained to me one day in his office that teaching was not as critical to the University as research productivity, and that he hadn't been as productive as his colleagues required him to be.

What I am hoping you get from all this is that even if your professors are passionate about teaching, most professors have to be careful about limiting the time we devote to teaching. In fact, I know of at least one large university in the U.S. where professors are routinely warned not to get any teaching awards before they are tenured. This is because getting such an award implies that those professors have not devoted enough time to their research. Professors often believe that good teachers are poor researchers. And because it's our fellow professors who decide whether we deserve to be tenured, we often have to cave into this pressure not to be great teachers.

The irony is that often the best researchers are very good teachers too. For example, in our Psychology Department here at Notre Dame, historically there has been a positive relationship between research productivity and good teaching evaluations from students.

So the first step in getting into the minds of your professors is realizing that we are not teachers by training. Unless you are at a very small college or community college where the professors do not have to publish their research, your professors are researchers first and are teachers second. Your professors are primarily committed to advancing knowledge with their research and publications. The teaching typically is more like an add-on of things they have to do.

WE LOVE THE ESOTERIC

The second step in understanding your professors is that as we become trained to do research, we come to love studying topics and ideas that most people would consider to be esoteric. And we come to respect other people who do the same. The professors who study basic, as opposed to applied, research questions get more respect. Likewise, the professors who study micro processes, such as microbiologists, get more respect than those studying macro processes, like ecologists. For example, a professor studying the digestive system of worms would get more respect than a professor studying how to increase recycling behaviors in humans.

Talking about who gets respect reminds of an instance years ago when a senior colleague told me as we were interviewing several professors for a position in our department, "The hallmark of a good professor is someone who is passionate about ideas." He felt that he could identify a good candidate for the position by how excited the person got when discussing ideas.

Indeed, people who end up being professors are particularly curious about ideas and are interested in trying to uncover the mysteries behind the many unanswered questions life presents. Perhaps this is why we get the label of being eggheads or absent-minded. We are willing to spend countless hours trying to get to the bottom of something that only very few people care about.

In fact, I am guilty of this egghead quality myself. For example, I have spent years trying to understand why when people present themselves to others in certain ways, they start to become the person that they presented themselves to be. I believe that a leading impression-management researcher Professor Barry Schlenker had it right when he said that it's because when people act in certain ways, and someone is watching, they become obligated to show some consistency in their personalities.[9]

In a project that I did with my former wonderful graduate student Robert Rodriguez to test this idea, we had undergraduate participants describe themselves as introverted in one videotape and as extraverted in another. We told them after they had finished taping themselves that we only needed to keep one of their two tapes to be viewed later by a group of counseling psychologists. Half were told that their introverted tape was kept and the other half was told that their extraverted tape was kept. They were told that this pick was merely random. The videotape that was not kept was erased in front of them. Then we asked them to wait in the waiting room. Our experimenter peeked into the waiting room, saw a person sitting there, and then asked the participant to carry a chair into the room because she supposedly had forgotten to put enough chairs in that room. It turns out the participants who had had their extraverted tape kept, as compared with those who had their introverted tape kept, actually sat an average of 14 inches closer to the person sitting in the waiting room, and they later rated themselves as more sociable. Thus, the participants who had their extraverted tape kept actually became more extraverted. We concluded that these findings supported the idea that simply thinking that someone (in this case, a group of counseling psychologists) is going to see us acting in a particular way obligates us to behave in a way that is consistent with how we think that someone sees us.[10]

Pretty interesting findings, no? If you did find them interesting, great, you will have an easier time making your professors love you.

But if you were bored reading it, which is much more likely, you're not alone. A few years ago, a producer from

ABC's 20/20 primetime news show called me in my office and asked if I had any interesting recent findings for the public at that time. I explained what I just told you, along with some other stuff our research team was doing on the importance of having an accepting confidant when disclosing secrets.[11] After listening impatiently, she responded in a shrill voice, "Do you have anything that isn't so *esoteric?*"

There it was. In that one instant, I was made aware of what a complete egghead I can be. Out of touch with the public. Head in the clouds. Grinding away at research that only a narrow group of people would show interest in.

What you can take from all this is if you express a genuine interest in what your professor finds interesting, or if you can show excitement around ideas that you want to investigate yourself, you likely will have a stronger relationship with your professor than will your classmates. Professors love ideas, and we love students who love ideas.

WE'RE INVESTED IN CREATING FUTURE PROFESSORS

A third step in understanding your professors is that we are committed to advancing knowledge as opposed to merely applying knowledge. This a key difference between professors and almost every other profession. The great majority of college professors have a PhD in their field. The PhD is a research degree. Professors must produce their own independent original work in order to get a PhD. In contrast, people who earn a medical degree, an MD, must learn a great deal of existing material and know how to apply that material. For example, a professor with PhD in biology could spend years studying how cholesterol causes the arteries to become blocked and lead to heart disease, whereas medical doctors would learn how to diagnose heart disease and what medications to prescribe to reduce the blockage.

As part of learning how to think independently and how to advance knowledge, we professors become committed to the pursuit of knowledge. This means that we are going to need new students to continue to advance knowledge after we're gone. When we spot a student who is like us – passionate about ideas, interested in the esoteric, committed to investigating unanswered questions in the sciences or humanities – we like that student and want to see that student succeed. In fact, if you show yourself to be this kind of intellectual student, you might find your previously disengaged professors starting to bend over backwards to help you land a top placement in graduate school. Perhaps *they* will ask *you* if they can write you a letter of recommendation!

NO ONE CAN OBJECTIVELY GRADE ESSAYS

If you do convey to your professor that you are this special kind of student who is interested in advancing knowledge, the advantage you will get from this impression is likely to extend to the grades you will earn. This is because much of the grading is not objective. Professors evaluate your class participation based on their subjective perception that you are contributing quality comments frequently enough. And they rarely grade papers blind. If they see your name at the top of the paper, and you are the kind of student who seems genuinely interested in ideas and in acquiring knowledge for its own sake, they will already be expecting you to get an A. Thus, if you happen to write some ambiguous or confusing sentences, expect them to give you the benefit of the doubt. They are likely to give you a higher grade than they would give a student who has not made this positive impression on them.

But shouldn't professors be completely objective when it comes to grading? Of course! However, research suggests that's impossible. Research has shown that when professors are evaluating the quality of a piece of writing, their preconceptions about the writers influence how they evaluate that piece.[12]

This reminds me of a time in graduate school when a professor said to his teaching assistant regarding grading papers, "I know in the first few sentences whether it's going to be an A."

After hearing that comment, I became determined not to fall into that trap as a professor myself. I always grade my students' papers blind because I can't help wanting to reward the students who have given great class participation with a higher grade on their paper than they might deserve. Yet I'm committed to being fair to those who haven't given excellent class participation.

SUMMARY

In a nutshell, to get inside the heads of your professors you must understand the following:
1. Professors are not trained as teachers, we are trained as researchers.
2. Teaching is often a hindrance to the research that your professors really want to spend time doing.
3. Professors love ideas and investigating topics that many people would find to be esoteric.
4. Professors are committed to advancing knowledge, as opposed to merely applying it.

5. Professors hold in high regard those students who are interested in acquiring knowledge for its own sake.

6. Professors will often bend over backwards to help students that they think will become professors.

7. Professors don't grade class participation or papers blind and can be substantially influenced by the impressions you convey regarding your commitment to learning.

Showing Your Professors, "I'm Here to Learn!"

Chapter 3

Now that you have a better idea of what is going on in the minds of your professors, let's get to how to convey just the right impression to get better grades and stronger letters of recommendation. Keep in mind as you read this chapter that if your professor categorizes you as a good student, she will likely give you the benefit of the doubt if something goes wrong, like if you accidentally sleep through a final exam. Good students are more likely to get the make-up exam; bad students are more likely to get a zero for the final.

GIVING THE RIGHT IMPRESSION

The ideal undergraduate student is both polite and active in class. This student is enthusiastic about learning and is curious about ideas, even esoteric ones. The student is very hardworking and conscientious. If you ever hear how professors talk to one another, we often say how hard-working we are ourselves and emphasize what long hours we put in. We want the same from our students.

The ideal student also is grateful to the professor and is cheerful, warm, and respectful of the others. This student comes to class early, sits in the front row, and demonstrates that she or he has done all the reading. When this student offers comments in class, he or she ties the comments directly to the reading for that day. The student offers critical analysis of the readings and integrates that analysis with what others have said in class. This last part describes the dream student in a seminar.

However, perhaps trying to come across this way might sound a bit calculating to you. After all, if you are strictly interested in business and sales, isn't it wrong to try to come across as being interested in esoteric ideas and research? That depends.

There was a case where a student's coming across as being interested in research did seem wrong to me. Once I asked a prospective graduate student to tell me about her future career goals during her interview for a graduate student placement in one of our doctoral programs. She and I both knew very well that our doctoral programs are designed to train students who want only to become professors, not to become therapists. But many students pretend that they want to be professors so that they can be admitted to the program and earn their PhD in order to ultimately open a private practice as psychologists. That's why I asked her about her career plans – to verify that she wasn't planning to earn a degree solely to become a therapist (there are other more appropriate graduate programs for training therapists). She responded to my question about her career goals by saying simply, "I love research."

I noticed that she shrugged her shoulders when she said the word *research*, but I brushed off the feeling that she was deceiving me because I wanted to believe her. Then, two years after she had entered the doctoral program she told me that she hated academia and that she had no intention of becoming a professor. Looking back, I believe that she had meant to deceive me in her interview by letting me believe that she wanted to become a professor. Thus, her response about loving research in the interview was wrong in the sense that later when she told the truth, I questioned her integrity. (Now I've learned to ask prospective graduate students directly, "Do you plan to become a professor?" And I play close attention to shoulder shrugs!)

In contrast to that student's behavior during the interview, what I am recommending that you do in your classes is not at all deceptive. You aren't going to lie and say that you want to become a professor (unless you actually do want to become one!). I'm recommending merely that you act as if you are truly interested in learning the material for its own sake. What you'll find is that after acting this way, you will actually start to become more interested. This interest is likely to develop even if you start out feeling as though you are feigning interest. This is because of that process I was describing in the previous chapter: When people present themselves in certain ways to others, they actually start to become like those presentations. So, if in front of your professors, you act as if you love ideas, are reading all the assignments carefully, and are interested in learning for its own sake; then you'll discover that you are all of these things.

29

OBSTACLES TO YOUR GIVING THE RIGHT IMPRESSION

This way of presenting yourself in class sounds simple enough, right? However, there are two main obstacles to your giving the desired impression described in this chapter: the other students and yourself. If it weren't for these obstacles, it would be so easy to be that enthusiastic learner.

If you come to class consistently prepared and eager to learn, coming early and sitting in the front row, you might feel the pressure from other students to back off on your enthusiasm. They might even call you a brown-noser or teacher's pet. In fact, occasionally I have seen students make fun of those students who participate actively in class, particularly in classes where lots of students are taking the class as an elective, as opposed to part of their major.

The other students can indeed be the biggest barrier to your presenting that ideal image for your professors. You may have spent years cultivating the impression among your friends that you are so smart that you can get As without having to study much. It's difficult suddenly to switch your image to that of a very hard worker, which is too bad because professors love to reward effort with high grades.

A solution is to sit next to and befriend other enthusiastic students who are motivated to give a great impression. They will serve as a buffer to any negative feelings coming from the weaker students in your class. They also will help your image because your professors will come to associate you with them. Keep in mind that we professors can't help but lump students into groups according to how strong you are academically. Those weaker students will end up serving as a comparison group that makes you and your new friends look even better.

Another way to overcome this barrier is to enroll in the honors program at your college if you are eligible to do so. Honors students typically want to make a good impression on their professors, and thus won't make fun of you for trying to impress your professors during class. I see this enthusiasm firsthand because every spring I teach an honors seminar to freshmen. I love this seminar because the students aren't afraid to put forward a positive, hardworking, interested-in-the esoteric image to their professors. Many of them even publicly thank me for my seminar after each class period, which never happens in my regular classes. In essence, the students allow one another to present a great image.

Another obstacle to making a great impression can be *you*. Once, I was advising an undergraduate student for her honors thesis project. This project involved our putting in long hours together. One night she gave me her computer disk, which I inserted into my computer, only to see that she had labeled her thesis file with the very negative title, "Feces Thesis." I was surprised by her negative feelings about the project and even more surprised (and irked) that she would let me see that negativity. It's one thing to be hostile about having to do a big project. It's a much worse thing to let your project supervisor see that hostility.

But students' expressions of hostility toward professors are common. Psychologists dating back to Freud have observed that people can sometimes transfer issues about authority that they have never resolved with their own parents onto other authority figures, including and especially professors. After all, professors have real power over your future with grades and letters of recommendation, so it's natural to feel some desire to challenge the authority of

31

your professors. Sometimes students will challenge their professors merely for the sake of challenging them or to assert a feeling of their own power. What I encourage you to do to avoid the risk of sabotaging your image is to try to get to the bottom of any angry feelings you might have toward your professors. Ask yourself if it is because they remind you of the injustices you have experienced at the hands of other authority figures. Freud believed, as do many psychotherapists today, that the more aware you become of what feelings and thoughts you might be suppressing, the less likely those feelings are to rule your actions.[13] This doesn't mean that you won't challenge your professors, especially when it comes to critical analysis of course material, it just means you won't stick it to them merely for the sake of sticking it to them as in the case of the "feces thesis."

SUMMARY

If you want to make a great impression on your professor, always come to class early or at least on time, sit in the front, look interested, ask insightful questions that follow from the lecture, and associate yourself with the top students in the class. Do everything you can to come across as being in class primarily to learn and express gratitude to your professor for that gift of learning. You will indeed be that Clever Student that gets the benefit of the doubt if any problems arise, gets the better grade if you are between two grades, and gets the very best letters of recommendation.

Handling Excuses for Missed Classes or Exams

Chapter 4

It wasn't until this year that I finally came to understand why students who were really sick or distracted would take one of my exams and then *afterwards* would ask me if they could re-take it. It's because nowadays when students have just finished taking the SAT or some other standardized test, they are given the option of not using their score and retaking it later. Therefore, you probably think that as long as you have not yet received your score on your professor's exam, you should be given another chance.

Yikes! Here is what your professor is likely to be thinking: "Why didn't you tell me about this problem before you took the test? You could have just seen that the test was harder than you expected, and then decided you weren't ready. Now you expect me to write you a make-up test when you have already seen all the questions?!"

You see, when we professors took the SAT, we weren't given the chance not to use our scores. So we have no clue that you might be expecting this courtesy. Plus,

33

we are not full of test questions so that we can easily give a make-up test like those people at the standardized testing agencies. And most important, we professors want to see ourselves as being fair to the other students. If we give you a make-up test after you took the test and bombed, it's not fair to all the other students who bombed and (appropriately) didn't ask for a second chance. This emphasis on fairness to the other students helps to explain the logic behind the rules to providing excuses that I describe in this chapter.

Before applying these rules for good excuses you should check your college's handbook for what they consider acceptable excuses for missing exams or classes. Typical university-accepted excuses are (a) documented illnesses, (b) funerals on the day of the test or class, and (c) athletic or other university-sanctioned events. These are just the typical categories of excuses that professors must allow without penalty to the students. However, professors have the discretion to be more flexible and to accept many more excuses for missed classes or tests. Thus, it's important to read carefully your particular professor's syllabus and see what procedures and excuses are considered acceptable.

Keep in mind also that your college dean has the power to override the rules and regulations laid out by your professors. For example, if you find yourself, and I hope you never do, in the position of losing a close family member during the semester, you should contact your dean's office immediately. Have your dean send an email message to all your professors to allow you to miss classes and/or tests for whatever duration you need to get back on your feet. In the next section, I explain the elements that go into a really good excuse.

FOUR RULES FOR HANDLING EXCUSES

The first rule in handling excuses for make-up tests or classes that you have to miss is to tell you professors well in advance or as soon as you possibly can. That means, for example, that as soon as you find yourself throwing up the night before an exam, you email the professor and say that you cannot make the exam because you are very sick. Leave a message on the professor's office phone too. Say that you hope your professor will understand and will be able to give you a make-up test. State that you are heading off to the infirmary and will contact the professor as soon as you are well enough to come back to class. To play it safe, you might also want to leave a message with your college dean because some professors might require excuses to come straight from the dean's office. This is especially true for final exams!

If you are too sick to do all that, then ask your best friend or roommate to contact your professor and dean's office as soon as possible on your behalf. The key is to act quickly, before your fellow classmates take the exam.

The second rule is to be ready to provide documentation. This rule might sound heartless or cold. After all, shouldn't your professors just believe you when you tell them that you have to go to a wedding or funeral and that you have already purchased your plane ticket? Yes, I always want to believe my students and give them the benefit of the doubt. However, I need to be and *want to appear to be* consistent across all my students. Only once in all my years of teaching did I slip up, and I still feel bad when I think of it. About 10 years ago, after having emphasized as usual on the first day of class that students had to show up for all three scheduled exams unless they had a University excuse, I let a student talk me into letting him go home a day early for Easter break because he had already purchased his plane ticket. Another student overheard and was very upset. That other student had booked a more expensive flight because he had assumed that he was required to stay for that Thursday's test. It would have been better for me to have stuck to my rules, which I have done ever since.

You might be saying to yourself as advice to me, "Well, just be flexible right from Day One, and then all your students will be happy." As you are saying that to yourself, do you realize what kind of chaos that could cause? Recent surveys have shown that most college students admit to having cheated at least once in college. If I let some students take the test early, it could tempt them or others to cheat by finding out from those students what was on the test. (Remember, we professors aren't full of lots of parallel test questions to draw from for each exam.) The bottom line is that I try not to tempt my students to cheat.

As I'm writing this, I'm reminded of an outgoing and funny friend who told me recently that when she was in college, she had bought a front-row concert ticket before she discovered that she had an exam on that same day. She told me that she lied to her professor by saying that she had to go to a wedding on that day. She then became disgusted when the professor did not believe her and made her produce a (fake) wedding invitation, which cost 100 dollars. Needless to say, she ended up not enjoying what turned out to be a concert that, as a college student, she could not really afford!

The third rule is to be sorry that you will have to miss the class or test. It is so sweet when students are sick and yet still muster the energy to say how much they love the class and how sorry they are that they will have to miss it. Students who do that really get their professor's sympathy and support.

The fourth rule is to keep it simple. Providing too many details can make you look guilty, because you are acting nervous and are going on and on about facets of your excuse that can look like a smokescreen. Too many details also can reveal that you *are* guilty, like the student I mentioned in the opening chapter who told me that she was throwing up because she had gotten too drunk the night before the test.

Too many details could prompt the professor not to give you the make-up test. One thing that students often have done in my classes over the years is call me the morning of an exam. They give me details of their illness and then ask if I think that they should take the test. As I am talking to them, they sound perfectly healthy. And they admit that they haven't been sick enough to justify going to the infirmary. This makes me think that they simply are in a last-minute desperate panic to get out of the test because they ran out of time to prepare for it. My mind immediately jumps to thinking about all those students who are not calling me to get out of the test. Again, I want to be fair to those other students. So I am inclined not to give a make-up exam when I'm handled by my students in this particular way.

A much better way to handle your professors, even really stern ones who are not inclined to give make-up exams, is for *you* to tell *them* that you are too sick to take the test. Don't put them in the position of trying to decide whether you are sick enough to get a make-up test. If you are well enough to engage in all that negotiating, they might think that you probably are well enough to take the test. Remember, professors don't like to give make-up tests, so don't put the burden of trying to figure out if you should have one on them. They will probably talk you out of thinking that you need or deserve a make-up exam.

EXAMPLES OF BAD AND GOOD EXCUSES

Let's talk through an example of a bad and a good excuse to illustrate further the four rules I have just described. If you want to share your own experiences in providing excuses, please post these on my blog at TheCleverStudent.com, so that other students can benefit from what you have learned.

A bad excuse. Around two years ago, a student emailed me shortly before spring break. She explained in her email message that she wanted to take her mid-term exam early because she had a medical school interview on the day of the exam. She also explained that she was anxious to keep that interview date because she had already moved the medical school interview to accommodate her trip to Cancun for spring break. Does this seem like a bad excuse to you? Why or why not?

In answering these questions, you need to understand that medical school interviews are in that grey area for professors to allow make-ups. They often are not in the category of typical university-accepted excuses, which as I mentioned earlier are (a) documented illnesses, (b) funerals, and (c) athletic or other university-sanctioned events. But many professors will excuse students for such interviews.

What made that student's request for a make-up not a good one is that she conveyed to me that her trip to Cancun was more important and less flexible than my exam. She conveyed this message after I had clearly explained both on the syllabus and in my lecture on first day of class that I viewed all three exam dates as being a commitment. I had told them that it was important to schedule all other events, including interviews, around these test dates.

My solution in this student's case was to say that I did not allow this type of excuse, but that if she could get an excuse from the dean's office, I would over-ride my usual policy. In the end, she just moved the interview. I was a bit relieved because I was able to avoid having to bend the rules for one student and risk upsetting other students who had dutifully scheduled their interviews around my tests.

A good excuse. Once, a student told me that stressors were getting so overwhelming for him that he could not concentrate on his studies. He told me how sorry he was to miss my class because it was his favorite. He even thanked me for getting him so interested in psychology. He then had a counselor at the University's counseling center talk to the dean's office about his case. The dean, in turn, sent a note to all his professors asking us to excuse him from all classes and tests for a 2-week period, and to give him make-ups when he returned. We were all sorry to see that he ended up dropping out of school. But had he returned, we would have gladly given him make-up tests and assignments even though his excuse of "overwhelming stressors" did not fit neatly into the university-accepted excuses. As you can see, his excuse was simple (i.e., without details that could undermine or embarrass him); he gave it ahead of time; he was sorry to have to miss; and he was thankful.

Your First-Rate Class Participation

Chapter 5

"Half of success is showing up...the other half is showing up on time." —Woody Allen

A recent UC Irvine survey found that a third of a sample of college students said that they should get a B just for showing up to class, and 40% said that they should get a B for doing all the reading.[14] Some experts blame this feeling of entitlement to good grades on a recent rise in narcissism among college students.[14,15]

But I believe that it's because some professors actually will give you a B just for showing up on time for every class and doing all the readings. This is particularly true for seminars where class participation is a large portion of the grade. Students pick up on today's norms of generous grading, and many professors cave in to the expectations of students. Most professors are familiar with the findings from study after study showing that the grades that we give you are positively related to the grades you give us. So, some professors grade generously to avoid getting poor marks from students at the end of the semester.

At the same time, many professors hold high standards and require their students not only to show up, but also to offer insightful critical remarks during class to get high marks. Your challenge is to use your social intelligence to figure out which professors require more from you, and then you can work harder to provide these professors your highest quality work.

Another challenge is to figure out exactly what they are looking for with your participation. For instance, I know two professors who evaluate how supportive and helpful students are toward other students during class discussion. Yet other professors don't give your interactions with students much consideration at all. In fact, one professor recently gave extremely high marks to two exceptionally insightful, critical, and active female students who talked so much that a male student formally complained that those women had "hijacked the class."

Fortunately, most professors will tell you what they are looking for both in the syllabus and in class on the first day. Listen carefully to what they want from your participation and give it to them. Don't assume that what worked for a previous professor will work with your current one. And if you find yourself in a class where one or several students dominate the discussion, don't give up and let them take over. Try to associate yourself with them by joining in the spirit of their critical commentary. As mentioned in Chapter 3, professors tend to lump students into groups of excellence. You want to benefit from the excellence of your group.

Despite the fact that professors vary in what they look for regarding class participation, there are some guidelines that are likely to appeal to most professors. To give first-rate class participation, particularly in seminars where discussion is typically a big chunk of the grade, I recommend that you focus on making insightful, well-thought-out remarks that are tied to the reading. You should provide these remarks every class period if possible and look for opportunities to integrate your remarks with ideas expressed by other students and/or the professor. The Clever Student realizes that both insightfulness and integration are critical to super-high marks for class participation.

I myself look for this kind of participation to give As to my students, and I explain this way of grading very carefully on the first day of class. But still some students don't read and offer comments that are not tied to the reading. Others say absolutely nothing for every class day.

I've tried very hard to get these super-quiet students to offer their comments in class. Yet they just won't. They are so shy that they cannot muster the courage to hear themselves say something in front of their classmates. This semester I got an opportunity to gain some insights into the thinking of these super-shy students because I now have a student in my lecture course who took my seminar last year and never said a word in class. Recently, I took him aside after class and asked, "I could have told you that you were going to get an F in my seminar for not talking, and you still wouldn't have said a word, am I right?" He smiled sheepishly and said, "I think that is right. I kept wanting to say something but I just couldn't ever find the right time to jump in." This sort of inhibition is particularly likely to happen in classes where the other students participate very actively. My solution has been to tell them mid-semester that I will start calling on them to help them out. That has helped somewhat, but hopefully you won't find yourself in this spot.

Next, I offer suggestions for your giving first-rate class participation, depending on what kind of student you are to begin with.

THE SUPER-SHY STUDENT

The Super-Shy or very introverted student has trouble finding the appropriate time to insert a comment during class discussion. These shy students are constantly worried about making fools of themselves in front of the class. They have trouble taking risks with their comments and overcoming their inhibitions. This kind of student is fairly common, which is not surprising given that a substantial minority of adults have a full-blown phobia surrounding public speaking.

If you are this kind of introverted student, I recommend that when you do the reading for your seminar, write out an insight that you had as you read. Then, plan on saying that insight at some point during the class discussion. Pick a time during class to offer it when it seems at least reasonably related to what is being discussed. Or you can wait until there is a lull in the discussion. You can say, "I know this isn't exactly what we were talking about earlier, but one thought I had when I was reading last night was..." And then you offer your insight.

Professors of seminars are particularly appreciative of those students who save the day with comments just when the discussion seems as if it's coming to a standstill. Thus, by picking a time when it's easier for you to jump in because no other students are talking, you offer the bonus of helping to keep the class discussion alive.

THE TALKATIVE BUT LAZY STUDENT

Most professors are grateful to students who are simply willing to talk in their seminar. Thus, extraverted students clearly have an edge over the shy students. However, this type of student can also be annoying by offering shallow comments and not contributing enough commentary that is tied to the readings for that day.

I have to admit that during my freshman year in college I fit in this category. I was so busy with morning and afternoon athletic practices, that I found it hard to do all the reading for even my most interesting seminars. But I felt that I could always manage to offer some useful insights once the class discussion got going, even if I hadn't done the reading for that day. Relevant, provocative thoughts on the topic would always race into my mind, and I was more than willing to share them with the class in my favorite history seminar. It wasn't until three years later when I asked that history professor to write me a letter of recommendation that she said that I had come a long way since that freshman seminar. When I asked what she meant by that she said, "It's just that you were thinking like a freshman."

Hmmm. Thinking like a freshman. What could that possibly mean? More to the point, what can you get from this message? It means that I was blurting out ideas merely to be provocative. I hadn't done the readings consistently, and I didn't give especially insightful input to the class discussion.

After that, I practiced suppressing my extraversion and thinking through what I wanted to say in class before I would say it. I would ask myself, "Is this comment the deepest I can go with my insights? Does it take into account what's in the reading and what my professor and

45

classmates have already said?" If the answer was yes to these questions, then I would raise my hand and offer the comment.

So, if you are an extraverted student who relies on your confidence and ability to talk to get you through a seminar, I encourage you always to stop and think about what you are going to say before you say it. Because you are fearless, you clearly have an advantage over the super-shy student. But you can run the risk of looking like a shallow, lazy student who is not particularly insightful. A critical professor will see right through your façade and will know that you haven't done the reading. A simple solution is to make sure that you have always done at least some of the reading carefully so that you can offer at least one well-thought-out comment. Wait and listen carefully to what the other students are saying and offer reactions to their comments. However, always have as your goal that you are trying to advance the discussion with your insights, rather than the goal of simply calling attention to yourself and to the fact that you are participating.

A quick, final point that I should make about extraverts is that they can be particularly suggestible or gullible. For example, recently a colleague of mine who is very much an environmentalist jokingly told a group of students and faculty that he had turned in his Hummer for his current Toyota Prius (a fuel-efficient hybrid) to cash in on the government incentives for driving fuel-efficient cars. The extraverted person next to me who knows this professor well said, "Really? He used to drive a Hummer?" If you're an extravert it might be tempting for you, too, to blurt out your confusion. But it helps you look smart if you can understand jokes from your professors and avoid interpreting what they say too literally.

Your First-Rate Class Participation

SUMMARY

Offering first-rate class participation represents very different challenges for students who are on opposite sides of the introversion/extraversion spectrum. The introverted student has to find a place to get in some contribution; the extraverted student has to censor some extraneous comments and dig deeper for insightful ones. In either case, it is important to think through in advance what you might contribute to the class discussion from your insights on the readings for that day. Tie your comments to the readings as much as possible and integrate your ideas with insights that have been offered by other students and/or your professor.

Writing a Great Paper
for that Professor

If you have ever told yourself that you are a bad writer because you've gotten some bad grades on papers, I want you to forget that for two reasons. The first reason is that even great writers manage to produce duds once in a while. For instance, a super-smart professor (and one of the best writers I know) got a C on a major paper when he was an undergraduate at Princeton University.

The second reason is what every great writer knows: Good writing comes from practice, practice, practice. If you don't have a lot of practice, you are probably not a great writer just yet. Colleges today have writing centers that are devoted to giving students tips on improving their writing and opportunities for practice. *Please* go visit the writing center at your college if you feel that you are behind on your writing skills.

In this chapter, I outline the basics of writing a great critical paper and offer tips for figuring out the nuances of what each professor wants. Remember from Chapter 2 that professors are not trained as teachers. Nobody has shown us how to grade a paper, and how we grade is left to our discretion. Translation: Your professors can grade your papers however they see fit.

This discretion and power over your grade can make you cringe when you consider the fact that many professors make grammatical errors themselves like saying "between he and I" instead of "between him and me." It can be difficult to swallow the notion that these are the very people who are making decisions about how good your writing is. But this misuse of grammar doesn't mean that professors aren't capable of making good judgments about how insightful you are and how well organized your paper is. So do your best to give them exactly what they say they want. If you miss the mark on your first paper, try hard to decipher the critical remarks they write on your paper.

TIPS TO KEEP IN MIND BEFORE YOU START WRITING

Different professors grade differently. Before you read my tips for writing great critical college papers, keep in mind that different professors emphasize different things when they grade. For example, I know one professor who uses a point system for grading critical papers. In this system, the students lose points for sentence fragments, run-on sentences, spelling errors, and grammatical errors. Under her system, they cannot get an A unless they have none of these errors *and* they have stated the alternative argument and explained why their own argument is better. In contrast, in my own grading system, I emphasize the quality of the arguments and don't systematically take points off for spelling and grammatical errors.

Such a lack of agreement about grading should not be surprising given the results of a study published two decades years ago in an *American Psychologist* article titled, "But the reviewers are making different criticisms of my paper!" In that study of more than 150 papers that were submitted for publication to various psychology journals, it was discovered that professors would say very different things about what was wrong about a particular paper. Worse yet, there was hardly any agreement among professors in their evaluations of whether the papers should be accepted for publication.[16]

Using a great paper as a template for yours. Because professors emphasize different things when they evaluate your papers, it would be very helpful to see what an A paper looks like to that professor. If you get C or worse on a paper, and you don't know what an A paper looks like, you likely won't feel that you deserved that grade (unless you totally blew off that paper). I say this because people need to get to a certain level of competence at a given task before they know what it is that they don't know about doing that task well. A way to find out what you don't know is to get your hands on a paper that your professor has deemed worthy of an A in a previous semester. Hopefully your professor will be willing to lend you one to use as a template for your own unique paper.

Research conducted by Professor David Dunning and his colleagues at Cornell University helps to explain why students with poor grades often don't feel that they deserve them. About 10 years ago, they gave undergraduates some grammar, logic, and humor problems to solve, and then asked them to rate how they compared with other students at Cornell. It turns out that those students below the 12th percentile rated themselves as at the 60th percentile, or as above average, despite their low scores.[17] Professor Dunning argues that students need to get to a certain level of competence before they can understand how bad their previous performance on a given task was. He says that this gap between students' performance and their perceived performance presents a dilemma for professors who try to assign appropriate grades. A solution is for professors to educate their underperforming students about what it takes to get an A on tasks like writing papers.

This research reminds me of what happened to my super-smart professor friend who got a C on his paper as an undergraduate at Princeton. When he went to complain to the professor who gave him the C, the professor responded by handing him an A paper from another student. After reading it, my friend said, "Oh, that's what a great paper looks like!" And he came to accept his C.

So, if at all possible, get your hands on a paper that your professor considers to be superb. It is so much easier to write your paper when you have a template to follow, especially if that paper has to be written in a particular style, like APA style (i.e., the style used for all articles in psychology journals). Note that when you ask your professor to recommend a published paper or to give you a paper from a previous semester, make sure you are clear that you only want to use it as a template for structuring your own unique ideas (as opposed to cheating and taking the ideas from that paper).

Follow instructions. Another point I have to emphasize before giving specific tips on writing a great paper is how important it is to follow instructions from each professor. Every semester I tell students not to put their names on their papers. Yet every semester about 30% still do. I think it's because they are just using their default habits for writing and turning in papers, which is a big mistake. Part of your being a Clever Student is being flexible and adapting to what your professor asks you to do. If your professor says that you can have other students proofread your paper, then have them proofread it. If your professor says that you may not work with other students on the paper at all, then don't. If your professor says that your paper needs to be exactly 8 pages long, make it exactly 8 left-justified double-spaced, numbered pages with 1-inch margins. Use this format unless, of course, your professor asks for some different format, and then give exactly the format that he or she requests.

WRITING A GREAT CRITICAL PAPER

Now we can finally get into the specifics of writing a great critical paper. Most college papers are critical papers, because your professors are trying to train you to think for yourself and to question the ideas put forth by the experts in their field. However, some college papers are creative papers where the goal might be for you to tell some unique, imaginative story with beautiful prose. What I have to say next applies specifically to critical papers.

Provide a catchy, interesting opening. The first step in a good paper is to grab your professor's interest while still keeping a professional tone. Keep in mind that your professors are grading a big pile of papers, so you want to catch their attention. They will be grateful to you for catching their interest during what is typically an extremely boring and tedious exercise for them.

The Clever Student

Structure the paper in the opening paragraphs. Next, tell your professor very explicitly what your main purpose(s) of the paper are. Let him or her know exactly what you aim to accomplish in the paper. For example, for a philosophy paper you might say something like, "The purpose of this paper is to demonstrate that love is a greater virtue than justice." Again, your professor is grading a pile of papers. He or she gets tired. You don't want her fishing for your purposes or for the thesis of your paper. The more it jumps out at her without effort, the better off you are. Then, highlight what particular ideas and evidence you are going to present in your paper that support your thesis. By highlighting the main ideas, you are defining the scope of your paper. Sometimes it helps to state also what topics will not be covered by your paper. The bottom line is that you must structure the paper and provide an overview of what is coming in the paragraphs to follow.

I have discovered that the majority of even the top students will not sufficiently structure their papers. When I've asked them later what prevented them from structuring their papers better and from telling me more clearly the purposes of their paper, they have told me that they were afraid to commit to a specific objective. They feared that being so specific would make their paper easier to criticize.

Keep in mind that you want your paper to be easily critically evaluated by your professors. If they find your purposes vague, you are almost certain to lose points. So yes, you are going to have to go back to the articles you have read in class and re-read some of them to write your critical paper because your paper has to refer to specific points from the articles for you to get an A.

Writing a Great Paper *for that Professor*

Make each argument. Now it's time to make each argument. The main point behind this assignment is to help you learn how to use evidence to make a critical, persuasive argument. Thus, it's necessary for you to be specific in using evidence from your readings to back your arguments. Some professors will let you use observations from your own life, or personal anecdotes, to bolster your arguments; however, some won't let you use them. You need to find out what they allow. Be consistent in your arguments with your opening to your paper as you move from one argument to the next. In other words, make sure you deliver what you said the purposes of your paper were.

Use transitional phrases that link your paragraphs. As you move from argument to argument, make sure that you use smooth transitions to let your professor know where you are going with the paper and how the separate ideas fit together. Transitional phrases at the beginning of each paragraph or section can be things like, "My first point is that...; my second point is that; my final point is that..." Make sure that you offer parallel phrases like first, second, third; rather than firstly, second, and third.

It also helps if you can tie each idea to your broader purpose for the paper wherever possible. For example, you might say, "The reason this second point is critical in supporting my overall thesis is that..." It's better to risk being redundant in your paper than to be unclear about how each paragraph fits into the broader purpose of the paper.

Provide an amazing conclusion. Now you should wrap up your paper with a terrific closing. The conclusion is an extremely important part of your paper because it helps to pull everything together, and because your professor will read it immediately before making a final decision about your grade. I often have found myself boosting my evaluation of a paper by half a grade right at the last minute because of a particularly good conclusion. Your conclusion should recap all the major points of your paper. It also must follow from the rest of the paper, which means you don't bring up new ideas or conclude something that you did not establish in your paper. Finally, it should remind the reader of the purpose of the paper and how the paper fulfilled its purpose. Give the feeling that your insights were meaningful and worthwhile. A great conclusion should leave the reader with a very clear take-home message.

Proofread the whole paper and correct any errors. The final step is to check and recheck the whole paper for its flow and for any typos. Most professors are likely to conclude that if you were too lazy to proofread your paper, then you were probably too lazy to have made good arguments. I once read a student's paper that two other professors and I had to grade. The paper was solid throughout until the ending where it had several typos like the word "shit" instead of "shift". Not surprisingly, the student received a less-than-solid grade from the other two professors.

THINGS TO AVOID IN YOUR PAPER

Okay, so I just showed you what you can do to make your paper great, but now I need to point out what to avoid. There are a few key mistakes that even excellent students make in their papers.

The first key mistake, as I mentioned earlier, is to be vague about the purpose of the paper. The second key mistake is just summarizing, as opposed to criticizing, the articles or books you read for that course. Yes, criticizing is much harder. You have to think for yourself, and you don't know if your insights are any good. But you have to take the risk and make those critical points, or else you won't fulfill the assignment.

The third key mistake is to make a straw-person argument, where you simplify an author's position just to be able to attack it. In contrast, you are supposed to make an argument that is based on an accurate perception of the reading material you are criticizing. I can't tell you how common this problem is! When students make straw-person arguments, they present the point that they are arguing against in such a superficial manner that they seem not to have understood the original argument. It is really important to impress on your professors that you understood the readings for the course very precisely.

The fourth key mistake is making an argument that contradicts findings presented in your class readings or contradicts your other arguments in the paper. Students often make arguments where there are data that clearly contradict them in their readings.

A fifth key mistake is saying that you don't believe the data and then basing your argument on speculation. It's one thing to say that the methodology of a study that you are criticizing is flawed, and thus the data should not be trusted. That is fine. But it's another thing to say that the data from the study are wrong, which makes no sense because data are simply observations that cannot be wrong. It is conclusions that researchers draw from their data that can be flawed, and thus are subject to criticism. So, if you disagree with a researcher's conclusions, make sure you say that the conclusions drawn from the data, not the data themselves, are wrong.

A final key mistake to avoid is writing a creative paper when the assignment is to write a critical paper. Make sure you understand which type of paper you are supposed to write, because the rules for writing these different types of paper are quite different. Whereas critical papers have to be well-structured and backed by specific observations from your readings, creative papers often allow for much more flexibility in the structuring and writing style.

But even when writing a creative paper, you might find that one professor will dock you a whole letter grade for having one or two sentence fragments or run-on sentences, and another professor will welcome these "writing errors" if they enhance the creative style of your paper. You have to figure out what matters most to that particular professor. Is it creativity and taking liberties with conventions in writing, or is it tight critical analysis with no grammatical errors? Once again, getting your hands on a template would go a long way in helping you figure out what you need to do to get an A.

CONCLUDING NOTES

If you do find yourself with a much lower grade on your paper than you were expecting, I encourage you to see your professor to try to understand what went wrong, especially if you have more papers yet to turn into that professor. You need to avoid repeating the mistakes from the first paper because professors get particularly irked by recurring mistakes. They expect you to absorb and use the feedback that they've scribbled on your paper.

Perhaps while you are in your professor's office you might even persuade her that your paper was better than she had first thought, and she might actually increase your grade on it. However, if you find that your professor still thinks your paper was awful, ask if it would be possible to see a paper that earned an A on that assignment. Again, you need to figure out what it is that you don't know. You can always tell when you are getting good at something – it's when you realize how bad you were at it before!

Something you might decide after having read this chapter is that you just don't care that much about writing great papers. Or perhaps occasionally you will simply run out of time to write a really great paper for a particular course. After all, it can be a lot of work to go back to the readings and look for specific points to support your arguments. Still, as long as you know what it takes to make a great paper, then I've met my objective with this chapter. What you choose to do with this information is, of course, up to you. Keep in mind, however, that A students try the hardest.

Handling Conflicts over Your Grades

My brother Andy attended the University of Buffalo and studied chemical engineering back in the 1990s. While there, he took a physical chemistry course with a good friend. Only two exams made up the whole grade for that course: a mid-term and final exam. His buddy scored lower than he did on the midterm and exactly the same as he did on the final. Yet the buddy got an A- and my brother got a B+ for the course. When Andy explained the situation to his professor, the professor responded, "Well, your friend showed improvement."

I hope you never run into such a ridiculous argument from any of your professors. However, you are likely to have the experience of just missing a higher grade by one point or getting a lower grade than you know you deserved in a particular class. The question is, "Do you go and see the professor and try to get the grade changed?" That depends on the professor.

The Clever Student

Some professors will actually threaten to lower the grade of any student who comes to complain about a grade. Others will simply not budge, no matter how good your arguments are. They might even make you feel bad by saying something ludicrous the way Andy's engineering professor did.

Like Andy, I too had an absurd encounter with one of my undergraduate professors. I missed an A by one point because of a mistake in the tallying of points, so I went to her office to remedy the situation. I showed her that I had received only one point for what should have been a 2-point extra credit assignment. She responded by simply saying, "I was very generous with the grading distribution." Yes, she had been generous – students who had scored in the D range were given Cs. But that had nothing to do with me or the fact that I had been shortchanged a point. She wouldn't budge and only seemed very annoyed with me. So I slunk out of her office feeling absolutely awful.

However, many professors actually will consider good arguments and will genuinely want to correct any mistakes in tallying points. They are open to changing a grade even after the grades have been formally submitted and have appeared on your report card. I put myself in this category. I have been happy and relieved when students have caught the rare miscalculation of points, and I have promptly changed their grades.

In terms of changing a grade not because of a miscalculation but because of a good argument, I have only changed a grade once in my 18 years of teaching. What follows is the one argument that has worked on me. About 5 years ago, a student in my seminar who had actively participated in class earned only a B- for the course. Her two papers were in the C+ to B- range, and I gave her B for class participation, which averaged out to the B- overall. Even though she had talked a lot in class, I had found her comments not to be as well thought out as other students' comments were. Thus, it was tough to give her better than a B for participation. When she came to talk to me about the grade after the semester was over, she said that a B in my course would mean that she would graduate Cum Laude (i.e., with honors) – with the B-, she would not. She also pointed out that I had said at the beginning of the semester that I would give students who were between two grades the higher grade if their class participation had been strong relative to their performance on their papers. I did give her the B.

Some professors will consider changing your grade simply if one more point in their course would make the difference between your graduating with honors or not. I personally would not change a grade for that reason alone. I would feel bad for the students who were in the same situation but respected my grading system and didn't come to ask for points that they didn't earn. Like many professors, I need to be given an argument that will allow me *to be consistent across all the other students.*

Many years ago, as an assistant professor at Iowa State University, I was asked by a student I was fond of to change her grade in my personality course from a C- to a B. Her sole argument was that she needed the change to keep her scholarship. I must have said something like "I cannot change your grade", because she later sent a very angry letter to my new Notre Dame office that said, "We all know people who say that they cannot do something, when we both know that they can." Of course when I told her that I couldn't change her grade, I had meant that I could not change her grade without being totally unfair to everybody else in the class. It's too bad that she could not understand that.

The bottom line to appealing to your professors for a grade change is that you typically must present an argument that will allow the professor to be consistent across all the students. Before you do that, however, you have to decide whether it's a good idea to see your professor about a grade change. You need to figure out if he or she is open to making such changes. You will gather this information about what they say on the first day of class about grading policies, what they put in the syllabus about grading policies, and what their reputation among students is for changing grades. Also, keep in mind that sometimes it's just not worth it to try to get the next grade up because you want that professor to write you a letter of recommendation. Seeing the professor about a grade change might make him or her less favorably disposed to supporting you with a strong letter.

Despite what I just said about being ready with a good argument, remember that some professors are willing to help you out if you tell them that the next higher grade will mean keeping your scholarship or graduating with honors. Do not lie, though, because they can easily check up on you! Depending on your college's honesty procedures, they might even be able to take disciplinary action against you.

In closing this chapter on grade changes, I leave you with a positive thought. As crushed as you might feel when you happen to miss the next higher grade by only one point, keep in mind that you likely have just *made* the next higher grade by a point in at least some of your other classes. These near misses and breaks wash out over your whole GPA (i.e., grade point average). The near misses will not make a difference over your lifetime. Letting professors see you get frenzied over that A- instead of an A could, however, hurt your precious letters of recommendation. So even though you might never forget that unfair grade you got in a particular class, just as I haven't forgotten mine, hopefully you can keep it in perspective and realize that it won't make any practical difference in the long run.

Differences between Small Colleges and Large Universities

Before reading this chapter, find out what kind of college or university you are attending or plan to attend. Is it a *Doctoral/Research-Extensive University*, or what used to be called a *Research 1 University*? These are universities that typically offer a wide variety of undergraduate programs. In addition, they give a high priority to research and receive tens of millions of dollars in federal support for research each year. Most important for your purposes, these universities are committed to graduate education through the doctoral degree, as opposed to committed to undergraduate education. In fact, they award 50 or more doctoral degrees per year across at least 15 disciplines. If you want to see if your university is one of these, you can visit http://www.washington.edu/tools/universities.html. Be sure to check out both lists of private and public universities to find out if yours is listed.

LARGE, RESEARCH-EXTENSIVE UNIVERSITIES

The reason it is important to figure out what kind of university you are attending is that if you are an undergraduate and you are attending a Doctoral/Research-Extensive University, your professors are likely to have very little time for you. This lack of time is due to the fact that most of them must obtain large grants from the government or from various foundations, and writing grant proposals takes a great deal of time. They also are under constant pressure to keep their research labs going with innovative studies. And they have to publish their findings in prestigious scientific journals or books to maintain the positive regard of their colleagues. Many of them also serve as editors for these scientific journals. Therefore, they have to spend heaps of time reviewing research manuscripts and making decisions about whether those manuscripts should be published. If someone at a cocktail party were to ask a professor at one of these universities, "So you teach?" the professor might get offended because that is like asking a housewife, "So you wash dishes?"

Whom are they doing all of this work for? They do it for their colleagues, which include other professors in their department and professors in their field across the globe. Their colleagues' opinions of them matter because they are the ones who decide whether the professors can keep their jobs and get tenured after six years of employment there. Their colleagues also decide whether they can be promoted to full-professor status after another five years or so of employment.

The bottom line is that because they are answering to their colleagues, they are not answering to you. Any time they spend with you is time away from their research and away from writing their grant proposals and manuscripts. So if you find yourself in a class with a really horrible professor and you are wondering how this could happen, now you know why. This professor not only was never trained to teach, but no one cares very much about how well he or she is teaching. Some of his or her colleagues might even be encouraging this professor not to be too stellar at teaching!

SMALL COLLEGES

Small colleges or universities that are not classified as Doctoral/Research Extensive are another story. At these places, undergraduates' opinions of their professors do carry weight. The students' end-of-the-semester evaluations of their professors can make or break a professor's career. Professors at these smaller colleges often teach four courses per semester, as opposed to professors at Research-Extensive Universities who teach only one or two courses per semester. The professors at smaller colleges also serve in various service roles around campus. For example, they might help with undergraduate advising, serve as the drama teacher, or help with the recruitment of new undergraduates. Their work environment is defined by giving undergraduate students access to them. The best professors often have students over to their homes for meals and spent tons of time with them outside of class. The professors who win teaching awards are held in high regard by students and other faculty alike. They tend to get tenured and promoted the fastest among their peers.

The chances are that you will have an easier time finding good teachers if you are at a smaller college. This is because small colleges tend to hire and grant tenure only to professors who are good teachers.

The Clever Student

PICKING A GOOD TEACHER

However, if you do find yourself at a major research university, you can still find some pretty good teachers. This is because many professors are conscientious enough to care about whatever tasks they set out to do, even if those tasks don't get heavily rewarded by their colleagues.

You have it a lot easier than your parents did when it comes to picking good teachers. In particular, you have access to the Internet, which is full of other students' opinions of every possible teacher you might run into. If the other students say that the teacher is a boring lecturer but gives easy As, then you know what you're getting. If, however, you are willing to risk a tough class to have an interesting teacher, you will know that from the Internet too. In this section, I offer tips on selecting the best teachers based on previous research on what qualities of professors have been associated with the highest marks from their students.

I should mention that you needn't worry that picking the most popular teachers would be at the expense of picking high-quality teachers. After all, research has shown that there is a strong correlation between students' ratings of the teacher and their actual learning.[18]

The one exception to the relationship between being popular and being a good teacher is the professor who gives easy grades, who might be popular only because he or she is easy. When picking a good teacher, first try to figure out if your potential professor is an easy or hard grader. If the professor is a hard grader but is still really popular, then he or she is almost surely great.

Research conducted by Professors Greenwald and Gillmore at the University of Washington supports this idea. After studying three separate samples of students,

70

they found a close correlation between the students' expected grades and their ratings of the professor.[19] These researchers then asked several professors to give higher grades to students in their classes than they had in the previous semester. Sure enough, their students gave them substantially higher evaluations in that semester.[20] Greenwald and Gillmore's conclusion about grading was that "If you give out lots of Cs and students think you are a great professor, you're probably excellent. If you give out all A and A minuses, and students think you're just OK, you probably suck" (p. 1209).[19]

Second, when picking a good teacher, try to assess how dynamic your potential professor is in the classroom, because dynamic professors who are high in extraversion are likely to be your best picks. Note that extraversion is a broad trait that includes gregariousness, energy, warmth, positive emotions, spontaneity, confidence, and assertiveness.[21]

A famous study conducted by Ambady and Rosenthal back in 1993 supports the notion that even nonverbally expressed extraversion makes for good teaching.[22] They selected 3, 10-second video clips with no sound from 1-hour sections of classes taught by 13 graduate-student instructors. These clips were taken of the start, middle, and end of class. Then nine female judges evaluated videos for the nonverbal behaviors of the teacher. It turned out that the judges' ratings of how optimistic, confident, dominant, active, enthusiastic, likable, and warm the teacher was in those brief clips correlated extremely closely with the students' evaluations of the quality of the section overall and the teacher's performance. The findings are particular amazing given that the clips were so short, there was no sound on the clips, the judges' ratings were taken early in the semester, and the students' evaluations were made at the end of the semester.

Those findings might seem too hard to believe, but they agree with the results from a later study on the personality traits of excellent teachers. In 2001, 351 undergraduates at Missouri Western University were asked to rate how extraverted and effective their professors were. Extraverted items included how energetic, outgoing, and enthusiastic the professor was, and how good a sense of humor he or she had.[23] Analyses examining the students' ratings of their expected course grade, their own age, their enrollment status, and the extraversion of professor showed that only extraversion predicted the effectiveness ratings of the professor. And it predicted these ratings extremely closely. These findings are interesting given that previous research had shown that professors' self-ratings of their extraversion were not associated with students' evaluations of their performance as an instructor.[24] In a nutshell, try to pick professors who are known to be enthusiastic, confident, dominant, and upbeat in the classroom.

USING YOUR PROFESSOR'S TIME

If you are at Research-Extensive University, you have to be careful about how you use your professor's time. A few years ago, a professor at a Research-Extensive University told me that the key to his getting top marks from his students is to "give the appearance of being accessible, without actually being accessible." Indeed, his students gave him really high teaching evaluations. They liked and respected him...and never saw him outside of class.

I had a similar personal experience with a colleague who is an extremely popular teacher at a major U.S. university. When he discovered that I had just had a baby, he listened to my baby stories with great interest and enthusiastically said that he would send a "care package" of information on the latest research on child care (his specialty). That care package never came.

You are highly likely to run into professors just like them who are so wonderful and dynamic that you will want to visit them during their office hours and get to know them outside of class. They will seem genuinely interested in you, but won't really be able to give you much access to themselves because of their other time commitments. I know that these professors can seem rather heartless and insincere. But what we can learn from them, and the many professors like them, is that it's important to know how best to use their time or if you should avoid them altogether.

Much of figuring out which professors do not really welcome contact from their undergraduates comes down to using your social intelligence. Be a Clever Student in interpreting their nonverbal cues because sometimes they claim to be accessible, even though they are not. They might seem to flinch when you try to set up a time to see them outside of class. Also, if they list office hours on the syllabus as "by appointment only", that usually means that they don't have time to see you outside of class.

If, however, your professors do list specific office hours for when they are available outside of class, try to see them only during those times. And be totally prepared for the visit. If you want to see them because you missed a lecture or two, make sure you get the notes first from a fellow student. Study those notes, and ask questions about gaps in your understanding of the material. Don't ask the professor for his notes or ask him to re-give his lecture. He might send you away until you've gotten the notes from somebody else. Or worse, he might tag you as a lazy student, and won't give you the benefit of the doubt if you happen to write a marginal paper for your next assignment.

DIFFERENCES BETWEEN UNDERGRADUATE VERSUS GRADUATE SCHOOL

As stark as the difference is between smaller colleges and major research universities, the difference is even greater between undergraduate and graduate school. When you become a graduate student, you are in the transition period between being a student and being a professor, so you really have to start thinking and acting for yourself.

When you become a graduate student in any field, you develop a close working relationship with at least one professor, your graduate advisor. You become something like a cross between an apprentice and a colleague of that advisor. Your advisor shows you how to do research in your field, with the goal of publishing your findings together, which helps your career as well as your advisor's career. Advisors also typically hope to help you become a professor, and you need publications to get a job as a professor.

However, many advisors are quite passive and let their graduate students take the lead in their own training. Thus, the key difference between the expectations professors have of you as a graduate student, as compared with when you were an undergraduate, is that you will show more initiative. Showing initiative means, for example, that you will take the lead in setting up meetings with your graduate advisor, come up with your own research ideas, tell your advisor when you want to defend your thesis, and tell your advisor which members of the faculty you would like to have on your thesis committee. (Note that this committee is the group of professors who determine whether your research is up to the standards in your field.) Even if your advisor is not especially passive, he or she will greatly appreciate your initiative because it means that you are close to being ready to become a professor yourself, which is the goal of graduate school training.

If in contrast to being this go-getter, you are a whiny, complaining, and needy graduate student who leans too much on your graduate advisor for emotional support or for ideas about potential research ideas, then you will be in trouble. Graduate students as a group tend to complain a lot, and professors know this. To some extent this complaining is to be expected because graduate students are learning to become independent thinkers. But this process can create a good deal of tension between students and faculty. I recommend that you do less complaining than your peers, so that in the end, your graduate advisor and other faculty members can write enthusiastically supportive letters for your first faculty position or other job.

As you can see, being a graduate student is very different from being an undergraduate, when you worried about memorizing a lot of course material to get an A. In graduate school, more emphasis is put on your capacity to think critically and creatively. After all, you are getting trained to advance knowledge in your field, so you have to be able to come up with research ideas on your own. Very little emphasis is put on grades in your courses. If you can come out of graduate school with top publications, and yet get Bs in your course, you are likely to be at the top of your graduate class and definitely a Clever Student.

A final word about being a Clever Student in graduate school is that flexibly reading the cues from your professors about what you should be doing and then delivering on their expectations is a key to your success. In fact, a study of a sample of 170 psychology graduate students at Yale University showed that professors' ratings of their graduate students' practical abilities were a far better predictor of the students' creative, research, and teaching abilities than their GRE scores.[1] Thus, even though I stressed the importance of taking initiative in graduate school, it's critical for you to demonstrate your practical intelligence by recognizing that sometimes you should seek the advice of and help from your professors. For example, once you have a good idea for your thesis project, you should seek the advice of your graduate advisor about whether he or she thinks it has a high probability of being published. You should also get his or her approval on particular thesis committee members before you ask them to be on your committee. Sometimes there are faculty rivalries that you don't know about, and it would be disastrous not to check this out first with your advisor.

So the bottom line is that when you are in graduate school, don't put your social intelligence on a shelf. It needs to be ramped up even more than when you were an undergraduate. Do as much for yourself as possible, and seek consultation from your advisor when it seems appropriate to do so. Also, it's tempting to seek emotional support from your advisor much as you do with your parents. But this is probably not a good idea, since they are much more like employers than parents. Instead, lean on graduate students who have been in the program longer than you for emotional support and to try to figure out what is expected of you. This way you can come to meetings with your graduate advisor very well prepared. You can be that dream graduate student that will make your advisor the envy of other faculty advisors.

SUMMARY

This chapter was made up of three separate, but related major points. The first major point was that you need to figure out what type of college you are attending – a major research university or a small college – because the professors at these places behave very differently with their students. Whereas professors at major research universities typically view teaching as a burden and try to minimize their time spent on it, professors at smaller colleges are there for the students. Because professors at the bigger universities are so focused on their research, you have to be especially careful about how you use their time outside of class. The second major point was that you can find good teachers not just at the smaller colleges but also at the bigger universities by looking for those professors who express extraversion in the classroom. The third and final major point was that the difference between being a graduate and an undergraduate student is enormous. When you become a graduate student, you are like a semi-professor. Thus, you have to think for yourself and take much more initiative than you did as an undergraduate. But whether you are a graduate or undergraduate student, you are bound to make mistakes. The next chapter focuses on common mistakes students make that can easily be avoided.

Eleven Things to Avoid

O ne time I was lecturing in front a class of 165 students who were sitting in a large dimly lit lecture hall, when I couldn't help but notice a student picking his nose. He continued to dig away, completely unabashed, as I looked straight at him.

The reason I mention this seemingly trivial event is that it made me realize that students feel anonymous when they are sitting among other students. Yet we professors can see you just as if you were sitting there alone. If you are aware of this fact, you can avoid some of the common mistakes that students make because they feel anonymous, when in fact they are not anonymous. Next, I describe what I have observed to be 11 of the most common mistakes that students make that can be easily avoided.

The number one mistake to avoid is showing up late for class, even if there are 200 other students in your lecture hall. You might tell yourself that coming to class just a couple of minutes late is no big deal. After all, you are an adult now, and you don't even have to come to class in the first place. But your professors will notice your lateness, even though there are so many other students in the room. They will mentally tag you as one of the irresponsible students that they would rather not have in their class. And if you ever happen to oversleep for an exam or need an extension on a paper, you are less likely to get a break from that professor.

The number two mistake to avoid is leaving class, especially a seminar, unexcused for any reason. Last fall, I noticed that among a seminar of 20 students, about half of them would leave the seminar at various points during the 75-minute class period. Simultaneously, while serving on the Faculty Senate at Notre Dame, I learned that professors across campus were outraged by this same kind of "disrespectful" behavior that was becoming commonplace in the classroom.

So, I asked my students why they would leave during class and what they thought of this growing outrage on the part of their professors. They explained that because they are adults, they should not have to ask to use the restroom or make a phone call. They were stunned to hear that their professors were having such a negative reaction to their behavior.

I then explained to them that because our seminar was discussion-based, as opposed to lecture-based, it was too disruptive for so many of them to take a break. As a compromise, however, I offered always to give them a 3-minute break halfway through the class period, if they could wait to use the restroom until then. I quipped that "my bladder should be the weakest one in here", so naturally they all agreed.

The number three mistake to avoid is looking bored or sleeping in class. Looking bored includes frequently checking the clock, sighing loudly, rolling your eyes, or having an impatient and uninterested look on your face. Again, the professor can see your bored face even if there are 200 other students sitting all around you. You'd be surprised to learn how demoralizing these behaviors can be to your professors. As you have just read in the previous chapter, the best professors express confidence and dominance in the classroom. If you want to get the best out of your professors, help them feel confident by looking interested!

This recommendation to avoid looking bored reminds me of a famous, funny experiment involving a trick that 12- to 15-year-old special education students played on their teachers. The students had been coached by an experimenter to make eye contact, smile, and look very interested in what their teachers were saying by sitting up straight. After some time, they were coached to stop these reinforcements. It turns out that when the students were offering the reinforcements, their teachers gave them much more positive attention and much less negative attention than when the students were not offering the reinforcements.[25]

The number four mistake to avoid is surfing the Internet, text messaging, talking on your cell phone, or reading the paper in class. This mistake is very similar to the top three mistakes because all these mistakes can easily get you tagged as a student who is not serious about his or her studies and is not conscientious. The scary thing is that you can get this label even if you are caught surfing the Internet only once.

The Clever Student

Let me explain. A famous personality researcher named Walter Mischel discovered around three decades ago that when people make judgments about others, like when your professor makes judgments about you, they do so in a very superficial way.[26] They notice the representative behaviors of a category, like surfing on the Internet during class to represent being an unconscientious student. They then string these behaviors together across time, like seeing you surf the Internet one time and seeing you text message another time, to determine whether you are a bad student. So, you can't give them even one opportunity to jump to this wrong conclusion about you!

The number five mistake to avoid is chatting with your classmates while the professor is talking because it is disruptive to the class, and because your professor is going to see you as being disrespectful. However, this one isn't necessarily quite as bad as the first four, because your professor might actually think you are talking about the course material. The professor might even call on you to ask you if you have a question, which can be very embarrassing.

The number six mistake to avoid is asking obvious questions that the professor has already addressed either in class or on the syllabus. The classic example is asking if certain material will be included on the test when the syllabus says it will be. This mistake represents the category of poor questions that students ask that make them look lazy or unmotivated. The poor questions also get your professors worried that an anti-work ethic will spread among your classmates – a negative environment that you helped cause with your apathetic questions. Remember, the impression you want to give is that you are anxious to learn and willing to work hard.

Eleven Things to Avoid

The number seven mistake is saying nothing when class participation is required. This mistake can be catastrophic if a chunk of your grade is based on participation. You absolutely have to find the courage to offer your contribution to the class discussion. You can't count on the mercy of the professor to give you a B just for showing up.

The number eight mistake to avoid is saying or asking "stupid" things in class because you haven't read the assigned reading. Now I know you don't expect me to use the word "stupid", but I couldn't think of a better word to capture when a student hasn't done the work and tries to cover it up. It's tempting to put in your two cents and to think up stuff to say on the spot. But you can't count on your outgoing nature to pull you through classes where the professor is taking note of who did and did not do the reading. Even if you are pressed for time, always try to do at least some of the reading and write down at least some useful insight from the part you did read. That way, you can offer something insightful and memorable to the class discussion and stay quiet for the parts when you don't know what you're talking about.

The number nine mistake to avoid is telling your professor that you did very poorly on the SAT or ACT. The reason you want to avoid sharing such information is that professors are total geeks when it comes to standardized testing. What I mean is that we place too much emphasis on test scores, whereas most lay people realize that intelligence cannot be sufficiently captured by these tests. Therefore, if you say that you had poor test scores, many professors will quickly categorize you as not worth investing a whole lot of time on because you don't have much academic potential. Why shoot yourself in the foot? Only mention your test scores if they are great (i.e., substantially better than those of the average student at your college), if they seem relevant to the discussion, and ideally if no other students are listening (because they are likely to see you as bragging).

The number 10 mistake to avoid is making fun of students who do participate in class. This is a killer. Years ago I ran into a problem when I taught a large Introductory Psychology class of students who specifically were not majoring in psychology. About a third of the way into the semester, the students had simply stopped responding to my questions. I couldn't get anybody to say a word in class. What had happened in previous class periods is that any one of three particular (male) students would raise his hand after a student had responded appropriately to my question. He would twist that student's words or say something sarcastic. It got so bad, that I tried to get those students removed from the class, only to discover that there was no rule against their behavior.

Anyhow, to the extent that you can encourage your classmates to participate and help create a supportive atmosphere, your professors will greatly appreciate you. And as I mentioned in Chapter 5, some of your professors will even make that helpfulness part of your participation grade.

The number 11 mistake to avoid is waiting until *after* you miss a test or fail to turn in a paper by the due date to tell your professor why you couldn't make the deadline. It is extremely important to communicate with your professor about problems, either emotional or physical ones, you might be having during the semester *but only if they will prevent you from completing assignments on time*. I can't emphasize enough how important it is to communicate with your professors as soon as possible in these situations. It's a rare professor who will make you turn stuff in on time despite your troubles. Plus, if you are communicating with your professor, you can find out what he or she expects from you in terms of documentation for your excuse.

In closing, I know and hope that all 11 of these points seem obvious to you by now. The main point to keep in mind is that a Clever Student recognizes that a professor appreciates a student who helps create a classroom atmosphere that is conducive to learning. The Clever Student does nothing to undermine this positive atmosphere.

As you read this chapter, you probably thought of many other things to avoid that I haven't listed. Gosh, these include bringing weapons to class, saying the F-bomb during class discussion, screaming at the professor, throwing things, etc. I didn't mention these because they are so rare and obvious, that they go without saying. However, there is a whole category of things to avoid called cheating, which is extremely common and is on the rise because of easy access to potential papers to plagiarize on the Internet. The entire next chapter is devoted to what to do if you are accused of cheating.

What to Do If You Are Accused of Cheating

So the unthinkable has happened. You have been accused by one of your professors of cheating. What should you do?

You might recall that as Co-Chair of the Honesty Committee here at Notre Dame, I've seen a number of mistakes that students have made that have gotten them on the wrong side of their professor's good graces. I've seen students get worse punishments by having a Committee hearing than they would have gotten if they had accepted the punishment that their accusing professor originally offered. But I've also seen cases where the student got no punishment because the professor's accusation was ruled by the Committee as unfounded.

Taking the right course of action to protect yourself can have important implications for your future. If you decide to accept a professor's accusation of cheating and sign a form that says you admit to cheating, then you typically get a mark on your permanent college record. However, usually the only time this mark on your record is relevant is if you want to become a lawyer or doctor (and of course, a politician) because medical and law school admissions forms ask you if you were ever found guilty of cheating in college. If you lie on that form and are ever discovered, you can be thrown out of your medical or law school. Graduate school application forms, however, do not typically ask about any cheating in college. So if you want to be a doctor or lawyer, there is more at stake when you are accused of cheating.

Let's get back to what you should do if your professor has formally accused you of cheating and asks you to sign some sort of honor code violation report. The first thing you should do is carefully read your university's policies and procedures on cheating. You might consider hiring an attorney to help you interpret these policies, especially if you plan on becoming a doctor or lawyer (because having a violation on your record could prevent you from becoming one). Next, you should contact the chair of your college's honesty committee, who is likely to be a regular professor, and bring him or her any evidence on your case. Ask the chair if he or she thinks it would be a good idea to bring the case to the honesty committee. Sometimes these chairs have the power to tell the accusing professor that there is no real case and can dismiss it. Often, however, these chairs try to stay neutral and will direct you to have a hearing if the case does not seem clear-cut.

Here's what I would tell you if you came to see me as chair of the honesty committee. If (a) you did it, (b) there is solid evidence that you did it, and (c) your professor is offering a punishment that is less than what your college's guidelines for punishments for cheating are, then you should consider going ahead and signing an admission of guilt. However, if any one of these conditions is not met, then you should consider presenting your case to be heard by your college's honesty committee.

These honesty committees are typically made up of several fellow undergraduate students and a couple of regular faculty members at your university. Even though you'd expect your fellow students to be compassionate and to want to give you a light sentence, often their hands are tied regarding sentencing. They are limited because they are supposed to follow the guidelines for punishment laid out in your college's handbook on rules and regulations. At Notre Dame, turning in a homework assignment that was copied in its entirety is considered to be a major, not minor, violation *even if the assignment was worth only 2% of the total grade*. Usually professors tell students that they will get a zero for that assignment and ask the students to sign a violation report, which means that they will lose 2% of their grade for the course. However, if the Honesty Committee hears the case and decides that a violation did occur, our guidelines say that we are supposed to be punitive and go beyond merely giving a zero for that assignment. Thus, our penalty is typically something like taking 15% off the top of your grade for the whole course. That's why it's risky to take your case to the honesty committee at your university.

Another reason why it's risky to take your case to the committee is that if the committee thinks that you have lied to them, this can be processed as a separate violation. Being found guilty of two violations can lead to much worse penalties. At Notre Dame, this penalty can mean expulsion from the University.

The Clever Student

Sometimes professors who believe a student has cheated will offer to give a penalty of a zero for the assignment without asking the student to sign a violation report. Typically, professors are not allowed to give a zero for an assignment or any other penalty for cheating unless they have followed their university's procedures for reporting and processing claims of cheating. If you know you have cheated and there is evidence of your having cheated, consider yourself lucky to have gotten off with just a zero for the assignment. I don't recommend calling your professor out on breaking your university's rules, because following the rules means you might have to get that mark on your record, which could be far worse than just a zero for that assignment.

Now you might find it strange that a college professor who is the Co-Chair of the honesty committee at Notre Dame is rooting for students to get out of cheating violations. I can explain. Cheating is rampant in college today, especially now that it has become so easy to cheat with papers and exams available on the Internet. In fact, students can hire someone online to write an original paper for them for $15-$30 per page. They get confused about how wrong it is to cheat because they see so many other students cheating. As much as I hate the fact that cheating goes on, I feel sorry for the few students who get caught. I believe that when they're older and have kids of their own, they will almost certainly regret having cheated in college and will wonder why they did it. I don't believe that the majority of students who get caught cheating are going to turn out to be unethical lawyers or doctors. But their violation will prevent them from those careers.

Also, I have to admit that I myself was unjustly accused of cheating in college. I had given my buddy my Spanish homework assignment to turn in for me because I had to leave class a few minutes early. He copied all my answers and then turned both our assignments in to be graded. When the professor saw that we got the same few answers wrong on the assignment, she formally accused both of us of cheating. Thankfully, he admitted what had happened and no case was pursued against me.

Still that experience has had a long-lasting impact on me. I am rooting for the students accused of cheating to give us on the committee good arguments for why we shouldn't believe that they cheated.

At the same time, however, I get just as annoyed as the next person when students lie straight to our faces or give us very poor excuses for their cheating. It stuns me when they get indignant because we don't believe them. In the next few paragraphs, I provide examples of good and bad arguments that have been used in cases I have witnessed.

The most common thing students have said as a defense is, "I am not a cheater." They then describe what decent people they are – people who would not be capable of cheating. The trouble with that line of reasoning is that we see good people cheat all the time. That argument does not address the fact that the cold, hard evidence belies their words.

A good (and successful) argument I heard one student use was that, with all due respect, the professor simply was mistaken in what he thought he had witnessed. The professor thought that during a quiz she copied from a paper that she had scribbled notes on prior to coming to class. But in fact, that paper was on something entirely different, and she had put it away once she realized that the in-class quiz had begun. We on the Honesty Committee believed her.

Let's take another example of a good argument. Imagine that a professor formally accuses you of looking at another student's paper during an exam. She says that she observed you looking and then discovered that you turned in answers that had similar mistakes as did that other student. You can explain to the committee that you were merely looking up because your eyes were strained from having put in an all-nighter studying. You can also explain that the reason you and the other student made similar mistakes is that the two of you had studied together and had ended up with a similar misunderstanding of certain parts of the course material. This argument might work.

Now this kind of argument won't work if you and another student turn in an assignment where you were supposed to work on the assignment alone, and yet you have similar and highly idiosyncratic wrong answers. There you can insist that you did not cheat, but no one on the committee can possibly believe you because of the implausibility of that idea that you each came to those separate, idiosyncratic conclusions.

Take the following as an example: Your professor for your Interpretive History class tells you that you must work on an assignment by yourself. Then 99 students turn in that assignment and get it mostly correct, including the fact that Columbus landed in the Americas in 1492. However, you and a friend both turn in very similarly phrased papers that say that Columbus really landed in the Americas in the early 1600s and base your interpretation of history on that "fact." Naturally the Committee has to assume that you worked together on that assignment, no matter what you say in your defense.

I have explained to students who were caught cheating that our Honesty Committee can use the implausibility (or even impossibility) of what they are saying in their defense against them, but they don't seem to understand that. Many students seem to believe that Committee members have an obligation to believe them even when the evidence indicates that they are obviously lying. They seem to believe that only if they admit to the cheating can they then be held accountable for their actions.

Please don't fall into this rut yourself. As a Clever Student, put yourself in the committee's shoes and understand what is possible to believe, and what is not. Don't make arguments that are impossible to believe.

The bottom line is that if there is no way that the honesty committee can believe that you didn't cheat, you should express remorse. Try to explain how you could come to do such a thing (i.e., the mitigating circumstances) and state that you will never do anything like that again. Usually committees can and will give lighter sentences if they can understand that the student was in an exceptionally tough spot and is remorseful.

In closing, I hope that all this advice is not necessary for you because you will never be accused of cheating. However, if you are ever prosecuted for cheating, try not to get too down about it and do your best to persevere despite what can be a traumatic experience.

Persevere is exactly what the late Ted Kennedy did after he got caught cheating at Harvard by having a friend take a Spanish test for him. Because of his cheating, he

The Clever Student

was expelled from the University and then sent off to war. However, even with such a negative mark on his record, he managed to re-enroll at Harvard and go on to having a brilliant political career. Perseverance is the key to overcoming so many obstacles in college, including depression, as I explain in the next chapter.

Overcoming Depression in College

Chapter 11

Y ou might find that as a Clever Student you understand very well how you should behave in college. You might be excellent at following instructions and reading the non-verbal signals from your professors. You may have mastered the art of giving first-rate class participation and writing A+ papers. But suddenly, like so many college students, you might find yourself experiencing mind-numbing depression just when you need to concentrate on acing your final exams. This chapter addresses how you can succeed even if you run into some serious emotional challenges during your college years.

Both fortunately and unfortunately, college is a time when your moods are likely to be particularly volatile. You are young, you are trying to fit in, you have tons of work to do to keep up with your studies, and you have very little cash. Your sex drive can be distractingly high while you are trying to concentrate on studying. You might have met your first love, and he or she might not love you back. You might not have been picked by your favorite sorority or fraternity. You might not know what you want to do with your life. You might be gaining weight because of all the food that is available at your dorm cafeteria and because of all the munching you need to do to get through your studies. All these things can build up and make you feel overwhelmed and downright depressed.

Why, then, would I say that it's both unfortunate and *fortunate* that college is a volatile time? This is because college is a time when you will likely experience not only bouts of depression, but also extreme joy and excitement. If indeed you are feeling low because of all the things I just mentioned, you are setting yourself up for feeling very good and possibly very soon. As strange as this may sound, these kinds of lows are necessary for you to enjoy the pleasures of relief and joy. We experience good moods because we recently have had bad ones, and through this contrast, we can experience happiness. Thus, we must have unhappy times to experience really happy ones. This is not to say that the lows that you experience from time to time in college aren't painful, because I know they are. It's just that bad moods don't last. Even if you end up crushed by a romantic breakup during college, research has shown that most people who lose their romantic partners ultimately find themselves at least as happy with their new partners.[27]

Not only do we need bad moods to experience intense joy, but negative events are likely to be more painful than our positive events are pleasurable. This is because we generally weigh negative events more heavily than positive ones. Researchers have discovered, for example, that in relationships, we need five positive events for every negative one to say we're satisfied. People can feel terrible about one tiny insult on a romantic date even if their lover has been nothing but kind and supportive all evening.[28]

I'm not saying that it isn't really nice to feel happy, just that it's even more intensely pleasurable to feel happy after we've been down because we can get accustomed to feeling good. Psychological research suggests that the key to attaining happiness seems to be finding ways of increasing the happiness in your life in small amounts at a time and to be able to keep doing that.[29] You would think that winning a multi-million dollar lottery would keep you happy for a long time. However, researchers found that a group of lottery winners was no happier than a group of regular folks within a year and a half after the win. Moreover, the winners were only a little happier than paraplegics who had experienced a debilitating accident with the past year. The lottery winners and paraplegics reported taking equal pleasure in mundane events and expecting equally happy futures.[30] This is because both groups had time to get used to their new circumstances.

So think of the down times while you are in college as setting you up to feel great about your good moods that are sure to follow, assuming that you are not suffering from either bipolar depression or clinical depression. If you have either of these, and I encourage you to check out this website http://your-ipc.com/index-2.html to read about the symptoms of each, then your best bet is to see a good therapist. A nice thing about college is that your student fees typically pay for some or all of the costs of seeing a therapist at your college's counseling center or health clinic. You should consider taking advantage of seeing a counselor while you are still in college, because after you graduate, you will need to pay over 100 dollars per hour for the luxury of seeing one.

If you do see a therapist at college and that therapist believes that you are clinically depressed, which means your depression has lasted at least two weeks, then he or she might refer you to your college's staff psychiatrist for depression medication. The rationale behind giving you medication is that elevating your mood with the drugs can give you the energy you need to get stuff done. Even if you are opposed to the notion of taking these kinds of medication, you might discover that they are just the boost you need. You can stop sleeping too long, get your dorm room in order, exercise more, and keep up with your assignments. After all, few things make depression worse than missing an exam or two and messing up your GPA (i.e., grade point average).

Sadly, occasionally college students feel so overwhelmed and hopeless that they take their own lives. Suicide rates are higher among college students than among young adults who are not in college.[31] Ironically, the students who end up killing themselves actually have a higher GPA and higher parental standards than students who do not.[31] However, they have recently had a drop in their GPA during the semester before their suicide.[32] Roy Baumeister, a social psychology professor at Florida State University, has argued that suicide represents an escape from seeing themselves in a negative way.[33] He says that these suicidal students just can't stand to see themselves as failures (and can't see that they are not failures).

Overcoming Depression in College

If you ever do find yourself feeling like a failure in college, remember that you are not alone. I can't tell you how many college students I treated when I was a therapist who said that they felt like failures because of a recent disappointing grade or two. Many of them said that they felt so bad because they had gotten all As in high school and had hoped to keep that same perfect record going. I encouraged them to see that they were being way too hard on themselves.

A famous psychologist named Albert Ellis concluded after observing many psychotherapy patients across the course of his career that people have a natural or biologically based tendency to be self-destructive or very critical of themselves.[34] A solution to this problem that had been proposed by another famous psychologist, Carl Jung, was to accept both our positive and negative sides.[35] In other words, we often need to lower our standards to stay mentally healthy.

So, if you do end up feeling terrible about failing a test or getting a poor grade on a paper, keep in mind that you don't need to be perfect. These occasional poor grades are not going to make a difference in the long run. You can still get into a good medical, law, or graduate school with some Cs in college. And if all your grades turn out to be not what you'd hoped for, remind yourself that you don't need to go on to a post-graduate institution to be a big success. For instance, Bill Gates dropped out of Harvard as a sophomore, and he didn't do too badly with his career (as the billionaire co-founder of Microsoft).

However, it might be just too hard to convince yourself not to feel bad about a failing a test or about being rejected by someone you love. You might have those feelings of wanting to escape seeing yourself in a negative light. And these feelings could cause you to drink too much, binge eat, sleep too much, or procrastinate on completing assignments.

One solution that often helped my therapy clients feel less like a failure when bad things happened in school was to work harder on their academic projects. As a rule, undergraduates tend to be huge procrastinators, pulling all-nighters in cramming for tests and writing papers. They often will drink at a party, eat lots of junk food, or see a movie whenever they feel like a failure. But you will likely discover that if you can get stuff done, you will immediately feel uplifted and less like a failure. When you find yourself feeling down because you have fallen short of some standard you have set for yourself, simply try to get something done. Perhaps you can finish a paper, read a chapter for a course, or study for a test. The key is for *you* to pick the thing to work on. Otherwise, the project will just feel like an additional burden. Then, once you're done with the project, you will feel better about yourself. You can then enjoy that party or movie even more because you won't be there to escape a negative feeling that you have about yourself.

You will be able to tell how healthy you are after a bout of depression because you will start to feel more hopeful about the future and, more simply, *you will be thinking about your future*. One of the observations that Professor Baumeister made when reviewing the data on people who make suicide attempts is that they become very fixated on the present moment, like focusing on the movements of their jaws as they munch on popcorn.[33] He says that it's as if thinking about the grander meanings of life would prompt them to think about themselves as failures, and they simply don't want to think. Once you notice that you are routinely thinking about events in their broader perspective, as opposed to fixing your attention on some relatively minor detail like whether your friend snubbed you at last week's party, then you will know that your thinking is getting healthier and more mature.

Talking about all of this reminds me of one of Eleanor Roosevelt's famous quotes. She said, **"You gain strength, courage and confidence by every experience in which you really stop to look fear in the face. You are able to say to yourself, 'I have lived through this horror. I can take the next thing that comes along.' You must do the thing you think you cannot do."** In essence, what maturity brings is courage and a broader perspective on our problems.

If you find that despite all this advice, college is just too overwhelming, depressing, and stressful, keep in mind that the emotional swings of your college days will get less and less profound. For instance, a study of 2804 people over 23 years showed that their negative emotions declined consistently over time.[36] As they mature, people generally become more humble, agreeable, emotionally stable, and conscientious. Those pangs of envy and inadequacy that you can so often feel in college are likely to become less frequent and less intense.

In conclusion, what I have emphasized in this chapter is that if you are depressed and want things to get better, see a therapist at your college. But if you don't want to see one, just wait and things probably will get better (just not as fast)!

Getting Your Professors to Write You Amazing Letters of Recommendation

Chapter 12

Naturally you want to land a great job when you're done with all your hard work in college. Or you want to go on to graduate, business, medical, or law school, and then get your great job. What few college students think about as they enter college is that they will need three very strong letters of recommendation from their professors. Yet *you* should be thinking about this now, especially if you are at a major university where most of your classes are large and your only contacts with teachers are in labs with graduate student TAs (i.e., teaching assistants). In this chapter, I offer tips on how to make yourself stand out to your professors, select your letter writers, approach them for a letter of recommendation, and help them write you an amazing letter.

The Clever Student

Before we proceed, however, I need to impress upon you just how strong your letters need to be and how important they are. You might think that saying that they need to be "amazing" is a little extreme. Wouldn't just a pretty good letter be enough to clinch your place in medical or graduate school? No, it likely wouldn't be enough, unless you have other noteworthy credentials to offset the lackluster letter. Do you realize how many amazing students are out there trying to land a spot in the top graduate programs just as you are? The letters that the successful applicants have are way over the top, with professors saying things like, "This is the best student I have had in my 20 years of teaching." If your letter says, "This student was clearly in the top 25% of the class", your letter will not help your case!

When letters have even one negative statement about a student, that student's whole application can tank. I once was puzzled by how a brilliant undergraduate student with extremely high GRE scores, nearly perfect grades, and extensive research experience did not manage to get accepted by even a single competitive doctoral program. I later discovered that one of this student's letters of recommendation had said that the student was intelligent and cooperative but did not seem to have the capacity to think well independently. The next year, when the student used different recommendation letters, the student got accepted by several top doctoral programs and even got a prestigious fellowship to one. This fellowship meant that the student got to go to graduate school for free for 2 years out of the 4 years!

I know, you're probably thinking, "How can I possibly prevent a bad statement in a letter about me?" Well, it's true that you don't have total control of how your letters of recommendation will look. This is of course because you are not writing the letter. It's also because you typically sign a form saying that you agree not to see what you recommenders say about you. (By the way, I recommend that you do sign that form and agree not to see the letter. Otherwise, you might seem paranoid, or your recommenders might object to writing a letter that you will see, or your letter won't carry as much weight because the admissions group will think that your writer was not able to be completely candid about you.)

Don't worry too much about what might go wrong, though. Let's focus on the surprising amount of control you do have in getting amazing letters of recommendation.

HOW TO MAKE YOURSELF STAND OUT

If you are at a large university, you might think you are at a disadvantage for having your professors get to know you. On the one hand, this is because your classes can be very big. There is no way for a professor to get to know you well enough in a big lecture hall to write you an amazing letter of recommendation. Yes, unfortunately it's this way even if you are the best class participant and even if you score the highest grade on the test. For instance, every year, a couple of students from my large lecture-based course, the Psychology of Personality, ask me for a letter. I tell them only to use me if they are desperate and know no other professors well, because my letter about them will be very short. All I can say in a letter based on my direct experience with these students is how well they did on my tests and if they asked any insightful questions during my lectures. And a short letter is not an amazing letter.

On the other hand, it is not necessarily the case that you are at a disadvantage for getting an amazing letter at a large university. This is because large universities typically have ample opportunities for students to get involved in research projects in labs run by professors. Find out how soon you can get involved in research so that you can start to develop a relationship with one of your favorite professors. Talk to other students who are doing research in various professors' labs and see which ones get the most attention and have the most positive experiences. Pick the most highly recommended professor's lab and then seek out this professor as soon as possible to see if he or she can add you to the research team. Be on time for your meeting with that professor and show great enthusiasm for that professor's research. Make sure that you have read at least one or two of that professor's publications. Remember, nothing is more delightful for a professor than a student who shares a passion for ideas, especially for that professor's ideas (see Chapters 2 and 3)!

Don't worry that this professor is not doing exactly the kind of research you are most interested in. What matters is the kind of training and attention you will get in that lab, especially the letter of recommendation you will get. Down the road when you apply for graduate placements, you can always make your research experiences sound relevant. This is because they virtually always are relevant. These experiences show your commitment to research and establish that you have been trained to do the kinds of activities that typically pertain to various graduate placements.

Usually professors are much more willing to give time to those students who work in their labs than to those students who are simply taking their classes. This is in part because of the norms of reciprocity, or the natural give and take of relationships. In other words, because you have been helping the professor with his or her research, that professor wants to help you land a graduate placement.

The bottom line is that if you can establish a one-on-one relationship with any professor, then later on that professor is likely to advise you on and help you get into graduate, law, or medical schools. That professor will get to know you personally and see you working with a research team, and thus will have more to say about you in a letter. Again, longer, more detailed letters are better ones. Professors are likely to feel more comfortable raving about how great their students are if they have had more contact with those students. It would be ideal if your professor ultimately advises you not just on your work in her lab, but also on an honors thesis project of your own. Then, the professor can comment on your initiative and creativity, on how well you think independently, and on how well you write. All these qualities are extremely important for graduate school.

One last thing that having a close relationship with a professor can give you is not so obvious, but can be super-important. This professor can potentially advise you which other professors tend to write really positive letters of recommendation for their students. You could get this information by innocently asking the professor that you are close to, "Whom do you recommend I get additional letters from? I am thinking about Professors X and Y; what do you think?" A professor who cares about you will nudge you away from getting letters from their colleagues who feel it's their duty to be brutally honest about the strengths and *weaknesses* of the students for whom they write letters.

Okay, so we've talked about how to get one great letter if you are at a big university. But you need three. What

I'm going to say next about getting two more letters of recommendation applies to you whether you are at a big university or small college.

You need to take at least some small classes or seminars taught by a professor. Even large universities offer these. These smaller classes will give the professor a chance to see how insightful and frequent your oral participation is and how well you write. Therefore, the professors of your small classes, as compared with your large ones, are in a better position to write you an amazing letter. Even if you have been slacking in your other classes, make sure you give these classes your best possible *consistent* effort. See Chapters 3, 5, and 6 on how to make a great impression, offer great class participation, and write great papers. If you make a strong impression and do exceptional work, you have now secured an additional amazing letter.

HOW TO SELECT YOUR RECOMMENDERS

When considering whom to ask for a letter of recommendation, you first need to consider who knows you the best. Take the three professors who know you best, and ask them to write you one. Again, this is because a short letter is a bad letter. If you approach a professor who only has seen you in his or her lecture hall, that professor will have very little to say about you.

Now you might be thinking that you have only had professors in big classes. You might be saying to yourself, "Can't I just ask a couple of them to write me one and give them my resume and tell them about me, and let them fill in the gaps in a letter about me?"

Certainly, some professors are willing to do this. If you find one who will, consider yourself fortunate. However, recommending students that they don't know well is likely to become less and less common as professors come to realize that we can be sued by a company who hires somebody that the professor had recommended who turns out to be a terrible employee. If a professor lies or exaggerates about how great a student is, that professor can be held liable for his or her deceptive comments.

Maybe you are in the opposite position where you have more than three professors who know you really well. That is much more likely to happen at a small college. Good for you! Now you have to think about which three to pick. There are four elements to consider as you make your choice, listed in the order of their importance:

1. Which professors will have the most and the most positive things to say about me?
2. Which ones will not say anything bad about me?
3. Which ones have the highest rank and/or are the most well-respected and famous in their field?
4. Which ones can I rely on most to get my letters in on time?

You will notice that I place more importance on the quality of your letter over the credentials of the letter writer. However, if you can manage to get a famous, well-respected professor to write you a long and extremely positive letter, then that would be the ideal letter to try to get. Often, though, the most famous and respected professors are the busiest ones who might try to get their TAs to write a letter for you. Or they might ask you to write it and then they will simply sign it. The trouble is that you are probably not going to write as strong a letter about yourself as would a caring professor who knows you well and knows how glowing the letters have to be for you to be competitive. I will have more to say about this later in the chapter.

You will also notice that I put a high priority on finding a professor who won't say anything bad about you in the letter. This is tough to determine, but one thing you can do is search your memory for all the times that professor has witnessed your behaviors. Have you ever been late for a class or meeting? Did you write one paper that bombed? Did you offer an in-class presentation that was sub-standard? If so, you might not want to pick that professor to write you a letter. Keep in mind that your professor is going to be asked to comment on your oral and written communication skills and on your reliability in your letter. Even showing up for one meeting late might be enough for that professor to rate you as only being in the 50th percentile for reliability. Thus, your letter would not be an amazing one. So pick a professor who has only seen consistent stellar performance from you. And if you can get that one professor who knows you best to tell you which professors to avoid for a letter, then you will really be in good shape. Certain professors have a reputation for not getting letters in on time and/or for commenting on students' weaknesses. The professor you are close to should know who these professors are.

HOW TO APPROACH A PROFESSOR FOR A LETTER OF RECOMMENDATION

Most students who ask me for a letter of recommendation will ask if they can meet with me about the letter. I gently tell them that this won't be necessary and instead ask them to provide me with lot of information about themselves, as I explain in the next section.

The trouble with meeting with each student who needs a letter is that often about 25-30 students will ask me for a letter right around the same time, between late October and early December. If I meet with each one, that won't leave me much time to work on their letters, given all the other activities I must also do for work. Plus, each student needs to have about 10 letters sent to all the different places where he or she is applying. And each one needs to be submitted individually electronically. So imagine me, and your own professors, having to spend all that time filling in our addresses and answering questions about you, along with uploading the letter we have written about you.

The bottom line is for you to be thinking about how you can make the writing of your letter of recommendation as painless and non-time consuming as possible for your professors. If you can manage to create this efficiency, your overworked professors will be appreciative. This appreciation is likely to translate into a stronger, more enthusiastic letter for you.

So here's what I recommend that you do. See your professor face-to-face, either before or after class or during office hours. Pick a time when your professor is alone and does not seem stressed out or harried. Say something like, "I absolutely love your class and was wondering, would you be willing to write me a strong letter of recommendation for XX (say what the letter is for)?" If the professor says yes, then say something like, "Thank you so much! I will go ahead and leave you my supporting materials in your mailbox tomorrow. Please let me know if you need any additional information."

There are four parts to this request that I encourage you to keep in mind:

(1) *Express appreciation to your professor for the great class.* This will make the professor want to help you, simply out of norms of reciprocity – you give a compliment, and

111

the professor gives a letter. And it won't seem like insincere butt kissing because it's natural for students to ask their favorite professors for letters.

(2) *Ask if the professor is willing to write you a strong letter.* The inclusion of the word "strong" is a little risky and unconventional because some professors are very territorial about the letters they write. They don't want to say whether the letter will be strong or not. However, I think that most of the time, and you will need to be a Clever Student to figure out when, it's worth the risk to try to get a read on how strong your letter will be. Asking this question might prompt the professor who would agree to write you a letter, but would write a bad one, to say that he or she can't write a strong one. In that case, you can simply thank that professor for being honest and let him or her know that you will ask someone else.

(3) *Express gratitude for the letter.* Acknowledge that you know how busy the professor is and that you are truly grateful. Professors are so overworked in the late fall. You kind words are the encouragement that they need!

(4) *Show that you are prepared.* Get your resume and all application materials together. This collection shows that you are organized and gives another concrete example of your conscientious behavior that your professor can comment on in the letter. In the next section, I explain what materials you should provide your letter writers.

HOW TO HELP YOUR PROFESSORS WRITE YOU AN AMAZING LETTER

I tell all the students for whom I write letters of recommendation what materials I need. I also tell them these materials will help me write them the best possible letter.

However, I've discovered that only a fraction of the students that I give this list to end up following all my directions. When they do, I get even more enthusiastic when I write their letter. And when they don't, I wonder why. I have come to believe that it's because they're so overworked with taking classes and filling out applications, that they use their default way of dealing with their letter writers, who usually do not ask them for anything specific.

So before you follow these steps, I strongly recommend that you listen to what your professors tell you that they need to write you a strong letter. Give each one exactly what he or she asks for, plus all of the following things that I list next in one big envelope with your name on it. Across the top of the first page of your materials you should write, "Information for Recommendation for YOUR NAME for XX (Law, Medical, Graduate) School. The first letter is due on DATE." Give this packet of materials to your professor (who has said yes already) approximately 4 weeks before the first letter is due. The reason I suggest giving the packet 4 weeks in advance is because if you give the packet too early, the professor might forget about it. And if you give it too late, your overworked professor might get annoyed. The materials to provide your recommenders are:

1. *A one-page brag sheet* where you immodestly tell them what you've done and awards you've received. If you've been away from school for a while, tell them what you have accomplished since you left. Be sure to include your GPA and GRE scores, but only if they are very good. The reason this brag sheet is better than your resume is that you are including sentences that they can just lift from your brag sheet and insert into your letter.

2. A statement of what capacities the professor has known you in and for how long. Indicate any grades you have received from that professor. This step is very important. You are trying to jog the professor's memory. After you tell them what classes you took from them and when you took them, you might say things like, "You wrote on my final paper for your senior biology seminar that, 'This was the most insightful, well-organized paper I have seen in years.'" You want to be specific. Again, you are trying to give them phrases that they can just lift and insert into their letter about you.

3. A statement of your career goals. If you are applying to graduate school, and there is any chance you might actually go into academia (i.e., become a professor), state this career goal loudly and clearly! Remember, professors bend over backwards for future professors. They will likely work much harder on your letter if they think you are aspiring to become one. And if you are applying to medical or law school, you might want to emphasize your noble career goals like, "I ultimately want to offer medical care to the children in those communities where families cannot afford health care." One thing that you must avoid, no matter what kind of school you are applying to, is saying, "I ultimately want to go into private practice." That sounds as if you said, "I ultimately want to make lots of money." Even if it's true, it's hard for any letter writer to get excited about someone who merely aspires to be swimming in cash.

4. A page with 2 columns labeled "Regular-Mail Letters" and "Electronic Letters". In the first column, list all the names of the schools that request regular mail submissions and provide the *complete addresses* of these schools. Do this even if the letter gets mailed to you because your professors have to include the school's address on the letter they write for you. In the second column, list the names of the schools that will be sending your professor an email prompt for their submission. With this complete list, your letter writers can later check to make sure that they have submitted letters for all your sites. For sites in both columns, mention what kind of program (e.g., doctoral program in clinical psychology, law school, master's program in social work) each one is so that your professors have the option to tailor their letters for the various sites. Mention the due date for each site, and list the sites in the order in which they are due.

5. For the sites that request paper mail recommenda-tions, *provide a set of envelopes with the school's addresses typed onto them.* Fill in each letter of recommendation form with your professor's information, not just yours. This will save them the time of tediously filling out their name and ad-dress over and over for the many letters they write.

WRITING YOUR OWN LETTER OF RECOMMENDATION

Sometimes professors put their students in the awk-ward position of writing their own letters for the professor to then sign off on it. They ask students to write their own letters partly because they are so overworked and partly because they realize that you know yourself better than they do. Thus, they genuinely think that you are better suited to write your own letter.

Now, at first glance, this sounds like a wonderful op-portunity. You can say terrific things about yourself and guarantee a great letter! The irony is, however, that stu-dents typically don't and cannot write a letter that is strong enough to compete with the kinds of letters that get students accepted to their dream schools. Remember, the best letters say things like, "This student is in the top 1% of students I have taught in 15 years." That is, they make quantitative, evaluative statements that give a sense of the qualifications of you relative to your peers. How can you possibly write something like that when you don't know even how you stack up compared to your classmates this year, let alone all previous years? That's my point, you can't.

But I do have some excellent pointers for you if you find yourself in the awkward position of having to write your own letter of recommendation. Keep in mind that when you get to this point, your professor has already said the he or she is willing to provide a strong recommendation for you. Your professor is pulling for you to do well, so don't be modest in your letter. In this section, I first explain the different critical parts of a very strong letter of recommendation, and then I give an example of how this kind of letter should look. Keep in mind that you are writing the letter from the perspective of your professor.

The opening paragraph. You should start by stating how pleased the professor is to be writing this letter for YOUR NAME for NAME of PLACEMENT and POSITION. You then indicate how long your professor has known you and in what capacity. You might say that in this letter, you will be addressing the student's excellent preparation and academic performance, along with your delightful personal characteristics that make you ideally suited for a career in XX.

The first few paragraphs. You should state what kinds of activities you have participated in that your professor has witnessed and those he or she has not witnessed that make you a great candidate. Comment on your excellent in-class participation and first-rate papers. Mention your laudable career goals and your commitment to those goals.

Amazing Letters of Recommendation

The next couple of paragraphs. These should address your personal characteristics. Make sure you use phrases like "insightful, self-motivated, creative, and brilliant" and "writes and thinks extremely well" for graduate schools, and phrases like "shows great honest and integrity, is extremely professional and mature" for law and medical schools.

The closing paragraphs. Here you want to recap the key excellent points about you. Say also that the professor gives his or her highest possible recommendation, with absolutely no reservations. Indicate how to contact the professor and that he or she welcomes any contact about this outstanding candidate (you).

Here's a sample letter of a very strong applicant to doctoral programs in clinical psychology:

November 22, 2010

Address of the School You are Applying To

Dear Colleagues:

I am very pleased to write this letter of recommendation for **Jane Doe**, who is applying to your graduate program in clinical psychology. I have known Jane for three years in multiple capacities: She was a student in my Psychology of Personality course, was a research assistant in my laboratory, and conducted her honor thesis research under my advisement. Thus, I know Jane very well.

I am not exaggerating when I say that Jane is in the top 1% of students with whom I have worked in the past 15 years. She is extremely intelligent, insightful, resourceful, hardworking, and organized. In my Personality course, which students complain is more difficult than their other courses, Jane had near-perfect scores on her exams and the highest point total of the 75 Notre Dame students. As you can see from Jane's transcripts, she earned 3.99 GPA here at the University of Notre Dame as an undergraduate.

Jane's research training and skills are also first-rate. She conducted her honors thesis research under my direction; and she worked in my research laboratory for 4 semesters, each time becoming more advanced in her participation. She led a team of 8 research assistants to conduct her honors thesis project. Thus, she already was functioning at the level of a second-year graduate student. She came up with the research idea and the design for the project that addressed the question, "Why do people who disclose even embarrassing secrets come to benefit from this disclosure?"

I was impressed by her having taken the initiative to apply for an undergraduate research grant to fund the project. She did indeed receive the money for a very well written grant proposal. This success in landing the grant did not surprise me because I had earlier read her proposal for her project for review by the human participants committee here at Notre Dame. In my many years serving on that committee, I have never seen one so well put together by a first-time applicant. She painstakingly provided the necessary details required for both the grant proposal and human participants' proposal with little direction from me. Thus, I know that she will be an exceptional graduate student, because she works extremely well independently, while also seeking and responding very well to constructive feedback. She is currently writing up the results from her thesis project for publication, and I am confident that it will be published.

Even though Ms. Doe is so competent as a student and researcher, she also is an excellent team player. For example, I would regularly discover Ms. Doe in the lab volunteering her time to help the other students with their projects at odd hours. This touched me because I could see that she wanted her fellow classmates to shine, too.

I cannot say enough about how wonderful Ms. Doe is as a person. She is extremely kind, thoughtful, modest, and brilliant. Plus, she sweetly appreciates the attention her instructors give her on her work. She has told me that she aspires to become a clinical psychology professor, and I see her as having tremendous potential to meet that goal. She loves to discuss ideas, and she integrates different findings and ideas with ease. She is highly creative and resourceful, too. For instance, she has trained herself on how to analyze her own data using both SAS and SPSS, which has come in very handy during our research meetings.

In closing, Jane is a superb applicant, and I give her my highest possible recommendation, with absolutely no reservations. I believe that Jane will someday make important contributions to psychology because she has all the essential qualities to do so. These qualities that she possesses range from being very insightful to being excellent at following through on the details that are necessary to develop a successful program of research. Thus, she is likely to be at the top of any graduate class and will be a joy to supervise. If you have any questions about Jane, please call me at YOUR PROFESSOR'S OFFICE PHONE NUMBER, for I will be happy to talk with you at length about her.

Sincerely,

Anita E. Kelly (YOUR PROFESSOR'S NAME)
Professor (YOUR PROFESSOR'S TITLE)

CONCLUSION

See? You do have more control over getting a great letter than you thought! I should mention that if writing such a glowing letter about yourself makes you feel too awkward knowing that your professor will be reading it, just tell the professor that you know that these kinds of letters have to be extreme to land a placement. The professor is likely not only to agree with you, but also to be impressed by how savvy you are to have grasped how these letters must be written.

Your Future Is So Bright

Chapter 13

As I was writing this book, a junior at Notre Dame came to my office to ask me to advise him on his senior thesis. I didn't know him very well since he had only been a student in my large lecture course, and my policy normally is only to advise students that have worked in my laboratory. In fact, I had never in my 18 years of teaching agreed to advise a student who only had taken a large lecture course from me. But yet I found myself happily agreeing to advise him.

What made him so different? Why did I make an exception for him? Basically, without knowing it, he applied virtually all the principles I have been suggesting throughout this book. For example, in my lecture course, he had asked insightful questions during and after class. He presented himself as extremely interested in ideas and research for their own sake. Then, when emailing me to set up a meeting about his thesis, he sent me a well-thought-out set of questions around a research topic that he had obviously spent a great deal of time reading about. During our meeting, he gave me the impression that he is passionate about acquiring knowledge and even about advancing knowledge. He told me that he originally had wanted to go into a career in international politics, but now he wanted to become a professor in one of the social sciences. Wow. What a Clever Student.

Toward the end of our meeting I couldn't help myself. I had to find out what made him so special. I said, "James (not his real name), you've managed me really well! How do you know how to talk to professors so well?"

After giving a modest little smile, James explained that his mom is a professor. Ahah! Naturally, he has benefited from a lifetime of insights into the life of a professor. He has learned from his mom what professors care about, how we think, and what annoys us about unmotivated students.

You are probably not so lucky when it comes to your social preparation for college. Very few students are. In fact, some of you have parents who never went to college. Or your parents went to college but might not have understood the social norms for college themselves. Most parents spend so much time emphasizing the academic-intelligence part, that the social-intelligence part gets skipped.

But here's why I say that your future is so bright. Unlike your parents' generation, you understand the critical role that social intelligence plays in your success, and you can cultivate and capitalize on this knowledge. Certainly there are extremely successful individuals with very high IQs like Bill Gates who got a 1590 on his SAT before the test was re-standardized and such high scores were even harder to get. However, there are plenty of extremely successful people who didn't score nearly as high on a standardized test of intelligence. For example, in the world of professional football, players take IQ tests to help their coaches place them in appropriate field positions. Quarterbacks are supposed to be the smartest players. Yet quarterback Dan Marino had one of the bottom IQ scores of his entire Miami Dolphins team. He also couldn't run well. But as most American sports fans now know, he turned out to be a brilliant quarterback who executed outstanding plays, read the plays of the other teams extremely well, and led his team to uncanny 4th quarter comebacks with great social skills.

My point here is to encourage you not to worry about how you did on your SAT. You know you can be brilliant in the classroom and ultimately in your chosen career. If you deliberately develop your social knowledge and flexibly read other people and respond to them effectively, and if you persist in developing your other talents, then you are very likely to succeed.[5] In fact, your professors are lucky to have you in their classes because you have taken the time to understand them. You are now prepared to manage them well and get in their good graces as they make decisions about what grades and letters of recommendation you deserve.

CONCLUSION

This book began with an assessment of your social intelligence in the classroom. It might be interesting to go back to Chapter 1 and retake the test to see if you can score close to 100% after having read all the chapters.

The rest of the book focused on getting inside the heads of your professors and offered tips on how to convey just the right impression in the classroom. There were specific details about how to handle excuses for missed assignments, write great critical papers, handle conflicts over grades, and get excellent letters of recommendation. I also provided pointers on what to avoid in college and how to deal with an accusation of cheating. The thrust of the book was to show you that there is much more to succeeding in college than being academically intelligent. The Clever Student is also socially and practically intelligent. He or she continually thinks about what is socially appropriate, reads the nonverbal signals from professors, is flexible in responding to what each professor demands in a course, is hardworking, communicates promptly with professors about problems with turning assignments in on time, is respectfully critical in class, ties insights to class readings, and is grateful and warm. The Clever Student understands that professors love esoteric ideas and findings, and they appreciate students who do too. Clever Students do nothing to undermine a positive learning environment and realize that professors can make lasting judgments about them based on only one or two observations. You've probably got the idea by now! Please share anything particularly valuable you've gained or any general reactions to my book on my blog at TheCleverStudent.com. Other college students and I are waiting to hear from you!

References

1. Sternberg, R. J., & Williams, W. M. (1997). Does the graduate record examination predict meaningful success in the graduate training of psychologists? A case study. *American Psychologist*, 52, 630-641.

2. Kelly, A. E. (2002). *The psychology of secrets*. The Plenum series in social/clinical sychology. New York: Plenum.

3. Jones, K., & Day, J. (1997). Discrimination of two aspects of cognitive social intelligence from academic intelligence. *Journal of Educational Psychology*, 89, 486-497.

4. Engstrom, C. M., Sedlacek, W. E., & McEwen, M. K. (1995). Faculty attitudes toward male revenue and non-revenue student-athletes. *Journal of College Student Development, 36*, 217-227.

5. Sternberg, R. J., Forsythe, G. B., Hedlund, J., Horvath, J. A., Wagner, R. K., Williams, W. M., Snook, S. A., & Grigorenko, E. (2000). *Practical intelligence in everyday life*. Cambridge, MA: Cambridge University Press

6. Ceci, Stephen J., & Liker, Jeffrey K. (1986). A day at the races: A study of IQ, expertise, and cognitive complexity. *Journal of Experimental Psychology: General, 115,* 255-266.

7. Gough, H.G., & Hall, W. B. (1975). The prediction of academic and clinical performance in medical school. *Research in Higher Education, 3,* 301-314.

8. Kosmitzki, C., & John, O. P. (1993). The implicit use of explicit conceptions of social intelligence. *Personality and Individual Differences, 15,* 11-23.

9. Schlenker, B.R., Dlugolecki, D.W., & Doherty, K. (1994). The impact of self-presentations on self-appraisals and behavior: The power of public commitment. *Personality and Social Psychology Bulletin, 20*(1), 20-33.

10. Kelly, A. E., & Rodriguez, R. R. (2006). Publicly committing oneself to an identity. *Basic and Applied Social Psychology, 28*, 185-191.

11. Rodriguez, R. R., & Kelly, A. E. (2006). Health effects of disclosing personal secrets to imagined accepting versus non-accepting confidants. *Journal of Social and Clinical Psychology, 25*, 1023-1047.

12. Brennan, D. J. (2008) University student anonymity in the summative assessment of written work. *Higher Education Research & Development, 27*, 43-54.

13. Arlow, J. A. (2000). Psychoanalysis. In R. J. Corsini & D. Wedding (Eds.) *Current Psychotherapies* (pp. 16-53.). Itasca, IL: Peacock Publishers.

14. Greenberger, E., Lessard, J., Chen, C., & Farruggia, S. P. (2008). Self-entitled college students: Contributions of personality, parenting, and motivational factors. *Journal of Youth and Adolescence, 37*,

15. Twenge, J, M., Konrath, S. Foster, J. D. Campbell, W. K., & Bushman, B. J. (2008). Egos inflating over time: A cross-temporal meta-analysis of the Narcissistic Personality Inventory. *Journal of Personality, 76*, 875-902.

16. Fiske, D. W., & Fogg, L. (1990). But the reviewers are making different criticisms of my paper!: Diversity and uniqueness in reviewer comments. *American Psychologist, 45*, 591-598.

17. Kruger, J., & Dunning, D. (1999). Unskilled and unaware of it: How difficulties in recognizing one's own incompetence lead to inflated self-assessments. *Journal of Personality and Social Psychology, 77*, 1121-1134.

18. D'Apollonia, S. & Abrami, P. C. (1997). Navigating student ratings of instruction. *American Psychologist, 52*, 1198-1208.

References

19. Greenwald, A. G., & Gillmore, G. M. (1997). Grading leniency is a removable contaminant of student ratings. *American Psychologist, 52*, 1209-1217.
20. Greenwald, A. G. (1997). Validity concerns and usefulness of student ratings of instruction. *American Psychologist, 52*, 1182-1186.
21. McCrae, R. R., & John, O. P. (1992). An introduction to the Five-Factor Model and its applications. *Journal of Personality, 60*, 175–215.
22. Ambady, N., & Rosenthal, R. (1993). Half a minute: Predicting teacher evaluations from thin slices of nonverbal behavior and physical attractiveness. *Journal of Personality and Social Psychology, 64*, 431–441.
23. Radmacher, S. A., & Martin, D. J. (2001). Identifying significant predictors of student evaluations of faculty through hierarchical regression analysis. *The Journal of Psychology, 135*, 259–268.
24. Feldman, K. A. (1986). The perceived instructional effectiveness of college teachers as related to their personality and attitudinal characteristics: A review and synthesis. *Research in Higher Education, 24*, 139–213.
25. Graubard, P. S., Rosenberg, H., & Miller, M. B. (1974). Student applications of behavior modification to teachers and environments or ecological approaches to social deviancy. In R. Ulrich, T. Stachnik, & J. Mabry (Eds.), *Control of human behavior, Vol. 3*, Glenview, IL: Scott, Foresman.
26. Mischel, W., & Peake, P. K. (1982). Beyond déjà vu in the search for cross-situational consistency. *Psychological Review, 89*, 730–755.

27. Baumeister, R. F. & Leary, M. R. (1995). The need to belong: Desire for interpersonal attachments as a fundamental human motivation. *Psychological Bulletin, 117,* 497-529.

28. Baumeister, R. F., Bratslavsky, E., Finkenauer, C., & Vohs, K. D. (2001). Bad is stronger than good. *Review of General Psychology, 5,* 323-370.

29. Baumeister, R. F. (1992). *Meanings of life.* New York: Guilford.

30. Brickman, P., Coates, D., & Janoff-Bulman, R. (1978). Lottery winners and accident victims: Is happiness relative? *Journal of Personality and Social Psychology, 36,* 917-927.

31. Hendin, H. (1982). *Suicide in America.* New York: Norton.

32. Davis, P. A. (1983). *Suicidal adolescents.* Springfield, IL: Charles C.Thomas.

33. Baumeister, R. F. (1990). Suicide as escape from self. *Psychological Review, 97,* 90-113.

34. Ellis, A. (2000). Rational Emotive Behavior Therapy. In R. J. Corsini & D. Wedding (Eds.) *Current Psychotherapies* (pp. 168-204). Itasca, IL: Peacock Publishers.

35. Douglas, C. (2000). Analytical Psychotherapy. In R. J. Corsini & D. Wedding (Eds.) *Current Psychotherapies* (pp. 99-132). Itasca, IL: Peacock Publishers.

36. Charles, S. T., Reynolds, C. A., & Gatz, M. (2001). Age-related differences and change in positive and negative affect over 23 years. *Journal of Personality and Social Psychology, 80,* 136-151.